The Tao of Poop

The Tao of Poop

Keeping Your Sanity (and Your Soul) While Raising a Baby

VIVIAN ELISABETH GLYCK

TRUMPETER
BOSTON • 2008

TRUMPETER BOOKS
An imprint of Shambhala Publications, Inc.
Horticultural Hall
300 Massachusetts Avenue
Boston, Massachusetts 02115
www.shambhala.com

9 8 7 6 5 4 3 2 1

First Paperback Edition
Printed in the United States of America

♾ This edition is printed on acid-free paper that meets the
American National Standards Institute z39.48 Standard.

Distributed in the United States by Random House, Inc.,
and in Canada by Random House of Canada Ltd

The Library of Congress catalogues the previous
edition of this book as follows:
Glyck, Vivian Elisabeth.
The Tao of poop: keeping your sanity (and your soul) while raising
a baby / Vivian Elisabeth Glyck.—1st ed.
p. cm.
ISBN 978-1-59030-287-3 (hardcover: alk. paper)
ISBN 978-1-59030-553-9 (paperback)
1. Infants—Care. 2. Parenting. I. Title.
RJ61.G53 2006
649'.1—dc22
2005018093

Of course, for
Zakary Alexander Koenigs (ZAK).

Your love has taught us
the true grandeur of life.

"Boarded the train there's no getting off."

SYLVIA PLATH
"METAPHORS"
(WRITTEN ON THE OCCASION
OF HER PREGNANCY)

Contents

The Tao of Poop

The woman down the block stops
To tell me about her 15-month-old:
He has two hundred words
in his vocabulary.
While she rattles percentages
and benchmarks I realize
it is only going to get worse.
There will be bumper stickers
to contend with and standardized
test scores to compare.

"Did you know there are flash
cards for infants?"

Flash cards?

"What does your baby do?" *she asks,*
as if breathing isn't enough.

STACEY GOLDBLATT
MOTHER OF TWO

Introduction

IF YOU'RE READING this book, you're probably in the thick of things right now. You've recently had a baby or you're expecting one. In short, your life is in the process of changing. You may even feel like the ground underneath you is giving way. I hope you'll take away two basic messages from this book. First, you already have all that you need. Trusting your intuition will serve you more than the latest parenting trend. Second, there's no escaping the poop—both literally and metaphorically. Much of parenthood is messy, challenging, and unpleasant, *but the hard parts of motherhood actually offer us the most potential for growth*. How we choose to deal with "the poop" will determine our experience and perhaps our children's as well.

I wrote this book as a way of collecting and sharing insights about the path of motherhood. Interspersed throughout the book are my stories and also the stories of other mothers who've come up against their own expectations, joys, and frustrations—and discovered valuable life lessons. I hope that our stories will help you to stay in touch with your own wisdom, your own authenticity, along this journey.

Each chapter includes a list of "sanity savers" and "thought exercises" to guide you toward the freedom that comes with understanding yourself and accepting your own choices in spite of, or in the face of, the stress, sleep deprivation, and worries you may be feeling. The sanity savers are practical suggestions from me and other mothers, ideas of what you can do to find balance in a job that often throws you off center. The thought exercises are lists of questions to help you to tap into your own inner wisdom. These questions can be answered in writing in a journal or they can just be contemplated.

Being a mother is the most joyous experience of my life. At the risk of sounding mushy, I can honestly say that being a mother completes me in ways that I didn't know were possible. Over and over, other mothers I've spoken with confess that the love they feel for their children is bigger than any love they've experienced before. They feel split wide open by this love.

At the same time, many of us have felt overwhelmed by the challenges of motherhood: trying to keep our precious ones safe; feeling responsible for their physical, intellectual, emotional, and social growth; sorting through the sea of information on parenting to keep up with the latest. Then there is the media to contend with—everywhere we look there are images of what motherhood *should* look and feel like, images that often just make us feel inadequate. The question is: As mothers today, how can we stay sane and true to ourselves?

I'm happy to tell you that we can find balance on this journey—and real wisdom. The challenges and intensity of motherhood can help us become more whole as individuals. Motherhood can help us evolve into more complete versions of ourselves—stronger, wiser, more resourceful, and fully connected to the power of our own love. In my experience, parenting is the ultimate spiritual practice. It wakes me up on a daily basis, commanding me to stop and pay homage to the ways of the universe. Above all, being a parent calls on me to finally understand that I am *not* in control—never have been, never will be.

In a way, becoming a mother is like having a big mirror placed in front of you, one that reflects all of your expectations, weaknesses, and strengths, as well as the limitless love you are capable of, love that was impossible to imagine before. This is the good news. Parenting can bring us face to face with ourselves in a deep, lasting way. And it can become an invaluable teacher.

Parenting has taught me, above all, to take a deep breath and just be with *what is*—whether it's frustration, tenderness, anger, helplessness, or joy. When the going gets tough—when the storybook scenarios of serene life with baby collide with the messy realities—I've learned to just stop and breathe. I watch the judgments I have about myself or my child; I observe them rising up within me. I remember that I'm not my feelings; I'm not this monsoon of fear or impatience or anxiety. When I stop and breathe, soon I see that I'm OK and my kid's OK, just as we are.

If we can become more aware of how things really are *in this very moment,* rather than how we want them to be, this parenting thing can become a lot more fun. We can actually learn to embrace and accept ourselves exactly as we are: the lousiest parent on the planet and the Divine Mother, all rolled into one.

• 1 •

Expectations are the enemy
of happiness

HERE'S THE TRUTH that "they" never tell you about becoming a mother: the first three months with baby at home can be a living hell. Why? To begin with, you've just given birth. You need sleep. And you've got some sort of postpartum "boo-boo" that has a not-so-subtle way of reminding you of the ordeal you just went through every time you get the courage to swing your legs over the side of the bed.

If you're among the 2 percent of moms who had serene water births listening to calming music, your partner behind you as you chanted Ommm, maybe you're feeling pretty good about the whole birth experience. But if you're among the other 98 percent of us, you've probably had the kind of experience that your child is going to be hearing about for the rest of his or her life.

I'll never forget the nice couple sitting next to us at breakfast not so long ago, as they watched my two-year-old son, Zak, and his toddler buddy, Jonathan, slowly wreck the restaurant. "We're going to start trying this month," they said as they longingly watched Zak plunge his arm into a gurgling fountain in an attempt to pull out someone else's wish money. "We're looking into options now. You know, home birth, midwife, no drugs."

I just nodded politely. I couldn't bear to tell her right then and there: *Whatever you've got planned, whatever script you're writing for this experience, it's not going to happen the way you expect.*

For most of the billions of babies born, the passage out into the light of day is accompanied by an equal number of tales of the raw and unexpected. Maybe you were like my friend Heather, who started out with a tranquil at-home water birth that rapidly descended into complications and a *quick* detour to the hospital. Perhaps, like my friend Pam, after eighteen hours of labor, your baby's watermelon-sized head induced a level-four tear that left you wincing each time you sat for the next six months. Then, of course, there's the emergency C-section after you have gone halfway through labor and the little guy crosses his arms and refuses to come out. Or, after years of trying, you finally bring home your new adopted baby, having gone through so much paperwork, red tape, judgment of your character, and scrutiny of your financial records to make it feel like a labor all its own.

In my case, I had the planned C-section, where the only thing that made up for having mammoth-sized staples in my abdomen was the fact that my husband and I did not have to go through the labor portion of our childbirth education classes. I will never forget the panicked and envious looks the other couples shot at us as we were excused from the class. They seemed to say, "Can we possibly get out of this too?"

All of this comes into play before we even consider the baby, whom of course, we must consider. I know this doesn't happen for everyone, but I fell madly, hopelessly, divinely in love the first second I saw my little guy. Immediately I forgave him for being a boy. The images of my perfect little girl floated away, back into the karmic waiting area to be bestowed on some other mama-to-be.

Before I got to hold him, the nurses dangled Zak above the curtain for me to see. After my first glimpse, they whisked his bloody little body away and slapped him down on a table like an eight-pound fish, where they began suctioning and cleaning him, despite his violent screams of protest.

"Good for his lungs," they said, as I lay helpless just three feet away. "C-section babies need to work their lungs to get the mucus out. Vaginal-birth babies do this in the birth canal."

After letting Zak bond with me for about twenty-five seconds, Daddy, nurse, and baby were off again, this time out of the room, for weighing and measuring. I lay there alone, with my legs feeling like tombstones.

Two hours later Mike came back to tell me that there was a little problem. Zak had developed a pneumothorax, or collapsed lung, and was now in the neonatal intensive care unit (NICU) in a bubble, receiving pure oxygen. Definitely not good news. In hindsight, after everything turned out to be OK, I realize it was pretty cool to have the NICU nurses teach me how to take care of Zak. Their relaxed attitude toward everything from letting a baby sleep on its belly to switching between bottle and breast was the start of my anti-supermom style of parenting.

One nurse told me in hushed, exasperated tones, "Nipple confusion is a farce. I've had thousands of babies in here who have no problem going from breast to bottle and bottle to breast." I tucked this information away for future use on some poor exhausted mother.

It's a good thing that bonding thing works between parent and baby. You see, Zak played the perfect little angel in the NICU. His lung repaired and began working normally within two days. The nurses all told us what a perfect, mellow baby he was. Inside, I knew it was true. He had slept a lot in utero (scaring me occasionally that something was wrong with him). I breathed a sigh of relief. This was going to be a cakewalk. Feed him every three hours, then he sleeps for three hours—what's so hard about that?

And then it happened. The very night we brought him home, the harsh reality hit, and for the next seven weeks I secretly wanted to find the return counter where I could bring this little guy and ask for a refund, or at least a little time off. My son could cry, nonstop, every day from 4:00 P.M. to 11:00 P.M. Amid his inconsolable crying and my desperate rocking, nursing, changing, humming, swaddling, pacing, sleeplessness . . . all I could ask myself was: Why would anyone do this twice?

I remember looking longingly at the happy, bouncing babies snuggled up against their mommies or daddies in the ubiquitous Baby Björns, thinking there is no way that I will ever be able to do that. Zak just cried and cried when I put him in a baby carrier. Far from looking forward to happy, bouncing times, I pictured myself strapping him in his car seat until he was twenty years old and driving in circles around town, blowing fifty dollars on gas, just to get him to calm down.

One night Zak screamed throughout the night. Mike and I took turns massaging his poor little tummy, which seemed to be aching so badly. We finally all fell asleep, spread across the bed in total exhaustion. Several hours later, I woke up and felt something kind of wet and sticky under me. It had a different texture from the buckets of postpartum sweat that came pouring out of me nightly. I felt around a little bit before I opened my eyes. *Hmmm,* I thought, *Do I really want to see this?*

When I finally opened one eye and peered down, I saw the end result of that terrible tummy ache. We were all lying in a pool of poop that had come flying out of Zak's diaper from both sides, soaking through our duvet cover, down comforter, and sheets, straight through to the mattress.

It made me think of the all-important task of decorating the nursery . . . remember that one? And getting everything in place? A wild nesting instinct overwhelms you from the first minute that the second line turns blue (or pink or whatever) on the home pregnancy test. So many moms I talk to spend countless hours getting everything "just so." There are innumerable trips to myriad baby stores to find the perfect crib, perfect sheets, bumper, comforter, borders, and more. My matching diaper holder sat neatly stacked with fresh newborn Huggies, the wipe warmer was plugged in, ready to go. All of that preparation was not coming in very handy as I lay in a pool of poop.

When Zak was about four weeks old (the height of hell), the gifts kept coming. People are so generous when you have a baby—it seemed as if there was a constant stream of UPS trucks pulling up with big boxes of great stuff. But mostly I remember the cards that came with the gifts. There was all this hoopla about babies being a gift from heaven, and baby boys being the best thing since sliced bread. I read and re-read these cards, looking for a small dose of reality, some indication that what I was going through was normal. But there was none, just cute little rhymes about the bliss we must be experiencing with our bundle of joy. Had the whole world gone mad?

How could my expectations and the reality of the situation be so incredibly far apart? Life as I knew it was gone. I felt mesmerizing joy just looking at my son when he was nursing peacefully; I had the oxytocin rush in a big way. But the seven hours of screaming a day was driving me nuts. None of the cards, gifts, or books told me what to do with this creature. I expected sleep deprivation, a feeding here or there in the middle of the night. But I did not expect to lie wide awake between feedings, waiting for the next whimper. I did not expect it to take three hours to settle Zak back down after a middle-of-the-night feeding, just in time for the next feeding. I did not expect to be walking around in such a blur that the slightest comment by my mother-in-law about my parenting would send me into a two-hour crying jag.

Who would listen to my truth? This was not fun! *When does the fun start,* I desperately wanted to know. How could my mother look so placid and have such a big heart while I sat in my room, my head buried in my hands, crying my eyes out because I was so exhausted and didn't know what to do? (Hint: Because not only had she given birth three times, but she'd watched her own kids become parents five times before.)

The inevitable conclusion I came to was that I was a bad

mother. My milk was bad. My son got tummy aches from it. Everything I ate was bad for my baby, which caused me to stop eating. (The plus side of this was that I got below my prepregnancy weight within five weeks; the negative side was that I was anemic and had no vital energy, and heaven knows what I deprived him of as a result of this self-imposed starvation—further proof that I was a *very* bad mother.)

When the fog finally lifted (and I started to get some sleep), it occurred to me that besides sleep deprivation, so much of my unhappiness was attributable to the fact that my expectations of idyllic life with baby and the reality of a newborn's needs were *wildly* divergent. My entire life I had longed for a tiny little creature whom I could nurture and call mine, but once he arrived I often wanted to run away. Moreover, the thoughts in my head were far from pretty, and I hid them from everyone, even myself.

The fact of the matter is that expectations are the enemy of happiness. Everything in our culture, from Hallmark to Babies "R" Us, teaches us to expect something different than what comes plunking out of the womb. If you're not careful, these expectations can set up a wild ride for the rest of your child's life—and yours too. First there are the expectations of how baby's health will be (a huge, nerve-wracking question), how baby will eat, sleep, poop, sit up, stand, walk, talk, run, jump. Then there are our expectations of who this person will be. If you peer deeply into your expectations, you'll find a whole, ready-made picture of who you hope your child will turn out to be, including his or her level of achievement in sports, in school, in professional life, and even his or her public contributions.

The first lesson that Zak taught me was to start letting go of expectations—of him and of myself. I would lock myself in the bathroom and repeat the mantra: "Breathing in, I accept. Breathing out, I let go."

I learned that it's OK to not like him every moment of every day. Moreover, I learned that when I just let him be who he is, rather than projecting my need for perfection onto him, pretty soon he ended up being the perfect little baby that I longed for, smiling and cooing and loving life. I'm not sure how that happens, but I do know that whatever it is, it's bigger than me and I should really trust it, because it works every time.

I discovered that I can alter my child's behavior by altering my attachment to my expectations. If I am fearful, he's fearful. If I am excited and optimistic, he's excited and optimistic. Our children sense our expectations and the projections that accompany them. Your attitude and behavior toward your child influences how and what he will learn and feel about himself and his abilities.

Letting go of expectations and how things should be is an immense gift that we can give ourselves and our children. It's far better than the best, most modern toy, or even that matching bumper and comforter (by the way, who is going to put a big, heavy comforter on a newborn? Zak's is hanging on the wall.)

But here's the biggest payoff: Learning to accept your kids exactly the way they are gives you a sneak preview of what it would be like to accept *yourself* exactly the way you are, sinking boobs and all. There's an entire capitalist system out there that survives by convincing you that this cannot possibly be true. The media are constantly barraging you with images of beauty that sharply contrast with your "new" postpartum body, so that on top of being in pain, sleep deprived, and confused, you can throw in a little self-loathing. (Why can't you be like that Hollywood ingénue who is back in size 0 clothing three weeks after having a baby, huh?) So this essential task of accepting the beautiful, wise, courageous you exactly the way you are, unshowered and reeking of spit-up, takes plenty of courage, meditation, and an effort to *not* buy the latest *Vogue* when you are three weeks postpartum.

Letting go of expectations means being present to what is, whether it's the throes of the baby blues, a living-room floor strewn with those perfectly adorable newborn outfits now stained with rotten milk and poop, or a heart that is about to burst with love at the magic of your creation.

These moments become part of the lore of your parenting experience, moments you will actually treasure forever as a rite of passage through the dark tunnel of your early days of parenting. As we all know, it's part of the wisdom you can impart to your girlfriend or sister or the woman in the grocery line who is about to have her first baby. Just do her a favor—tell her the truth and let her know that expectations are the enemy of happiness.

Thought Experiment:
Observe Your Expectations

What expectations of yourself or your child do you constantly come up against? Are you supposed to be a supermom? Are you determined to maintain your professional career without feeling guilty about it? Did you leave your career to have a family and now love your choice, or do you feel caught in between? Did your child come out completely different from what you expected or longed for?

Write down the expectations that you currently have of yourself or your baby. Reread this list often and add to it. What expectations can you let go of? If you can't let go of them, can you just observe your tenacious grip on them and separate yourself from your expectations? In other words, can you be present to your expectations without being attached to them?

What kind of freedom does this bring you? How do you think that letting go will affect how you parent? How do you think that letting go of expectations will affect your child?

[*Sanity Savers*]

Here are a few tips for letting go of expectations and just plain old coping.

1. Throw out any agenda you have the first few months. This time will pass so quickly, you'll forget that you couldn't take a shower for three days in a row or couldn't get out of the house until 4 PM.

2. Go easy on yourself. You are undergoing a major life change, and this is the tunnel you have to go through to get to the light on the other side.

3. Find humor and laugh at all of the things you absolutely cannot control. Don't take yourself so seriously.

4. Stay present and in touch with what's important right now. The next feeding, the laundry, cutting your toenails when you have five minutes. You'll get back to the rest of your life soon.

5. Absorb the serenity of your sleeping child. Breathe in the total release of their state of being. Synchronize your breathing to theirs. Use this as your meditation.

6. Read *Operating Instructions* by Anne Lamott. It's a raw, funny, joyous, horrific account of her first year with baby, and you will know that you are not in this alone.

7. Start writing. The book *Writing Down the Bones* by Natalie Goldberg is a great tool to get you started. Journaling for even five minutes a day will save your sanity and remind you that you do have a soul. You'll notice patterns when you go back and reread what you have written.

8. Remember to breathe. Inhale. Exhale. Make time to sit and just breathe for ten minutes each day. Even if it's in the bathroom. Even if it ends up being

only five minutes because the baby wakes up from his nap. Mantra: *Breathing in, I accept. Breathing out, I let go.*

9. Sleep whenever you can. Send your partner on a drive with the baby. Use earplugs and an eye mask—tune out the world. When you get the chance to sleep, take it. Let whomever is taking care of your baby take care of your baby. Baby will be fine. You won't be if you don't sleep.

10. Get help: Find a lactation consultant or a doula, hire a mother's helper, ask a friend or relative to come over, talk to other mothers, cry (a lot) to your best friend.

What She *Didn't* Expect When
She Was Expecting

JINI BERNSTEIN ARCHIBALD, 41,
MOM OF LEIGH, 3

When I hear that saying "The apple doesn't fall far from the tree," I often wonder, "Why doesn't this seem to apply to my child?" My mother tells me that, as a child, I was an extremely happy, social being who laughed easily and was excited about everything.

So why is my three-year-old daughter such a serious, cautious, and extremely sensitive child with an often unapproachable demeanor? She is nothing like I expected her to be.

When she was only a few months old, people would come up to us in stores or in the park and smile at her, expecting a cute baby smile or a sweet baby glance. All they received was a scowl or an averted gaze. Even the babysitter told me she was the most serious baby she had ever cared for!

To this day, when a friend says hello, my daughter often looks away or just doesn't answer. For a long time, this embarrassed and even disturbed me. I was upset that she wasn't "normal" and didn't interact like a typical, well-adjusted child. Deep down, I questioned my parenting skills, thinking that her shy personality meant that I was doing something wrong or that she was going to grow up unhappy and isolated. I had always envisioned having a child who was more like me. In fact, when I was pregnant, I pictured myself with a happy, playful, rough-and-tumble boy!

One morning during coffee with my girlfriends, I broke down in tears. I was emotionally exhausted and had hit a wall. My husband was out of town and I was completely focused on my daughter's "unhappy demeanor," our lack of ability to separate, and my fears of placing her in a social setting without me.

Since then, I have made gradual steps toward finding some balance in my life. Difficult as it has been, I now realize that my daughter has her own distinctive spirit and personality. And that reminds me that she isn't "mine." Rather, she is "hers" and "herself." I am learning to accept, nurture, and embrace the person she is, rather than trying to turn her into the person I wanted her to be or thought she was supposed to be. Of course, there are still times when I just want to push her forward and say, "Go play with the other kids. Laugh and be free!"

But I know that expecting her to be like me isn't the answer and will only push her further inward. It's one of the toughest lessons I've ever had to learn, and in fact it's my own child who has been my best teacher. The funny thing is, as she starts to find her own place in the world without my imposed expectations, she is showing signs of confidence, happiness, and self-reliance . . . and that makes us both happy.

· 2 ·

Other moms don't need help— and other lies we tell ourselves

A sudden rush from the stairway,
A sudden raid from the hall!
By three doors left unguarded
They enter my castle wall!

They climb up into my turret
O'er the arms and back of my chair;
If I try to escape, they surround me;
They seem to be everywhere.

HENRY WADSWORTH LONGFELLOW
"THE CHILDREN'S HOUR"

MY FRIEND MARGOT was a latecomer to the playgroup, the "new kid on the block." I remember so clearly meeting her when both of our children were just five months old. We connected right away as we plopped down on a blanket and started a conversation that seemed to shut out the rest of the world. We agreed we would meet again the following week for the Stroller Strides workout demonstration.

For those of you who don't know what Stroller Strides is, it looks deceptively like a gentle Mommy & Me workout. I had watched the long lines of women jogging and pushing their kids in those easy-to-maneuver jogging strollers up a big hill right by my house. "Oh," I thought, "they look so ridiculous. Why don't they just go to the gym and get a real workout? I wouldn't be caught dead doing that."

But then the day came for me to be a good sport and try Stroller Strides with the rest of the playgroup. I carelessly didn't eat anything before I left the house, wore my worst sneakers, and showed up looking for the party. By the time we were halfway through the class, I was ready to cry. For one thing, my butt hurt badly from the "real" workout I had done the day before at the gym. And I was heaving at the exertion of running and pushing my kid in the stroller, stopping to do twenty push-ups, followed by running up and down a flight of stairs fifteen times.

In the meantime, the instructor was shrieking instructions at the top of her lungs while she jogged past me with her two kids in a stroller. "Shhhhhh," I hissed under my breath. She was a mother, for God's sake—didn't she know that my kid was sleeping and giving me a fifteen-minute break so that I could get through the darn class? No way was my son going to sleep with that drill sergeant yelling in his ear. Besides, nothing on her jiggled as she jogged. In my mind, this made her most untrustworthy.

By the time we rolled back into the parking lot where we had started from, I was clear that this was my first and last Stroller Stride. Way too hard. My back hurt, my lungs hurt, and, most of all, my pride was injured.

While I was still bent over trying to catch my breath, Margot bounded over to me. "Did you like that?" she asked.

I looked at her incredulously. "No! I feel like hell. Why, did you like it?"

"Oh, yeah," she said. "I'm gonna join. Do it three times a week. Gotta get back into shape." That's when I realized that my new friend was supermom extraordinaire.

Margot had dropped out of the workforce after having

her first baby. Before that, she was the vice president of human resources for a prominent biotech firm. Her husband and she had just relocated to southern California for his work. At that point, she couldn't work part-time anymore and decided to stay home with her son, Nathan.

We became fast friends. We were both more than a little driven and had a lot in common. We were both from the East Coast, we both rolled our eyes at the constant baby-poop chatter all around us, and at this point, we both thought we knew exactly how to raise our children. Of course, most of the time, we did end up talking endlessly about baby poop and frenetically consulting each other about whether we were doing the right thing. It was so frustrating, we just couldn't stay off the topic!

Margot took on parenting as though she were trying to get a promotion at it. I always felt two steps behind her on most parenting issues. She had the best teething rings, the best intellectually stimulating interactive toys, and I was always dawdling behind her, shamelessly mimicking her hard-studied purchases.

Of course, I was a "working" mom, and although my office is in my home and I was working part-time, I always felt judged by Margot because I hired a nanny. I remember asking Margot to call off the dogs when she asked me how it was that Zak was learning English when our nanny was Russian and he spent all of his time with her.

"Margot, you're hurting my feelings," I said—after completing a defensive recitation of my schedule, the nanny's schedule, and Zak's schedule, making it clear that, in fact, I was spending hundreds if not thousands of hours more per week with my son than our hired help was.

Of course, she understood and apologized for pushing my "inadequate mother" button. But I always felt judged, as though I was just not putting enough time into this Zak-raising thing. I was left feeling that I couldn't possibly stay as informed about all the ways to raise the most brilliant, perfect, gifted child as I needed to because he was not getting 100 percent of my attention.

It wasn't until Margot's second baby was born that I finally understood that the whole time that I was feeling judged by her, she was really judging herself. She had a clear vision of the kind of mother she wanted to be, what she expected of herself, of her body, and of her kids. She felt a real need to prove to herself that she could and would do this mothering thing perfectly on her own.

When she was three weeks postpartum with the second baby, she met us for a walk. I'll never forget the sight of

Margot with her newborn strapped to her chest and her toddler in the stroller, pushing the two of them up a monster hill while carrying an overstuffed backpack. She had just had a C-section. All I could think of was my ob-gyn imploring me not to do anything more strenuous than picking up the baby until six weeks after my C-section was performed.

It was about that time that things began to unravel for Margot. In the few minutes that I could get her on the phone between sleepless nights, feedings, diaper changes, and struggles with her screaming toddler, she just seemed to be beating herself up. "I am so impatient with Nathan," she would lament. "I can't get Abby to sleep through the night. My body looks like hell and the ob-gyn tells me it is not going back to where it was."

Sometimes it just sounded like self-flagellation, and I would implore her to go easy on herself. "Just be with this, Margot," I would counsel as though I knew anything at all. "Be with your feelings, don't try to change them or muscle them into submission. You think you're supposed to be good and patient and kind, but unfortunately you're just being human right now, dealing with the adjustment to this new life. You're having a hard time. That's OK. It doesn't mean that there's anything wrong with you."

"You're right, you're right," she would tell me. "Just keep telling me this stuff. Eventually I'll get it."

But the situation seemed to be getting worse. She told me that she would spend the free time that she had crying about what a bad mother she was and lamenting how she was turning into her own mother, the last person she wanted to be. She told me that one time when her kids were asleep, she got into the shower and sat crying for twenty minutes so no one would hear.

Almost six months after Abby was born, she finally told me, "I was diagnosed with postpartum depression when Abby was six weeks old. My doctor has been begging me to go on antidepressants, but I've been trying the naturopathic way so I could keep nursing. It just isn't working, though.

"So many times I wish that it was just me and Nathan again. Not that I don't love Abby, but I just can't handle this. I can't handle it."

I thought about all the times I had grilled myself, wondering if I should quit working and spend every minute with Zak like she was doing. I thought about how hard I rode myself for not. I thought of the constant guilt that runs a big tape loop in my head, telling me that I'm going to regret it when this time passes. I will look back forlornly on the missed opportunity to create an Excel grid of all of the best preschools in town and evaluate them side by side against my son's special talent for pulling all of my underwear out of the drawer three times a day.

Watching Margot's Herculean efforts to raise her kids pretty much single-handedly, I often wondered, "Were we ever supposed to do this parenting thing all on our own?"

Why do we have such a hard time asking for help? Why do we feel so guilty when we want to feel like a human for a few minutes and take time for ourselves? I think a lot of women in this generation have trouble asking for help. We were taught to be independent, to live life with a can-do attitude, no matter what the personal cost. But knowing your limits is actually a strength, as is asking for help. Once you accept and understand your limitations, you can work *with* them. If you struggle against them, they will get in your way, which is what they do when you try to pretend they are not there. Your limitations can actually be your strengths.

For example, I know that I function poorly when I'm even mildly sleep deprived. Recognizing this early on in motherhood, I made it a priority to teach my son to sleep well. I even went so far as to track down a neuroscientist who could help me figure out where Zak's sleep cycle was amiss. We got Zak to sleep twelve hours a night and take regular naps. (I was so impressed with this woman's work that I've helped her write a book that will help other parents to get the rest they need, too.)[*] By recognizing this weakness of mine, rather than ignoring it or just "toughing it out," new learning and opportunities opened up.

From what I can tell, God intended for us to have at least one other generation living with us, with our siblings close by, not spread out continents or worlds apart. If God wanted us to raise kids all by ourselves, she wouldn't have given us parents. And if she really wanted us to *start* having kids in our late thirties and early forties, she wouldn't have made our eggs so juicy and ripe for fertilizing at age sixteen. But today, we're having kids later, our parents are older and less able to pitch in, and in many cases, they live on the other side of the country anyway. (You've listened to enough of their complaining about this fact, so I won't pound it in anymore.)

In "olden times" if we didn't have our mothers and sisters nearby, how could we ever go off by ourselves to wash our hair in the stream? How could we work grinding grains, gathering nuts and berries to create food for the whole tribe, all the while chatting with the other moms

[*] See www.90MinuteSleepMiracle.com for more information.

about our baby's poop? Someone else had to help us some of the time so that we didn't go stark raving mad. In fact, if God wanted us to raise our kids all by ourselves, she would have given us Prozac in our bloodstreams, right from the start.

So many of us are trapped in the supermom myth, the one that says do-it-yourself parenting is a badge of honor, the one that lets us feel self-righteous about ourselves even though it completely deprives us of time to take a shower, let alone having ten minutes to sit down and talk to a friend about something besides poop.

We tell ourselves, "I should be able to do this myself." But often we're ready to burst from the conflicting feelings of our expansive love for our kids versus our desire to just spend a night alone, with no squawking coming from the baby monitor at the crack of dark.

I remember Margot told me, "It's not more time for my husband I need, or more time with either one of the kids. I just need time for *me*. I'm the only one here who isn't getting attention. I've got to get some space to take care of myself so that I can come back and take care of them."

Sure, there are other moms out there who make it look easy, mostly because no one likes to admit that they can't handle the pressure. It's easier to keep it all in, and when we're ready to explode, we vow that we'll do better next time.

I say, let yourself off the hook. Whether you're working in the house, outside the house, or on top of the house, life is a hectic, nonstop barrage of details and "gotta-dos." If you're anything like me, you're constantly ignoring this overwhelmed feeling and telling yourself that you can tough it out, that your kids need you there all the time. And if you're anything like me, you've got an automatic timer in your brain that lets you know that the daily time allotment for your kid to be watching *Dora the Explorer* has just expired, so you'd better stop blow-drying your hair, stop reading your e-mail, stop trying to buy the perfect potty seat online, and go teach your kid something useful, for God's sake.

Whenever I can, I take time for myself, and although I feel the requisite amount of guilt the whole time, I still do it. For example, I do a big "me" thing once or twice a year. I find a local hotel room on Priceline for $40 to $80. (Almost unbelievably, my husband is very supportive of this.) I bid farewell to the family at about 6:00 P.M., go have a nice dinner either with a friend or by myself, check into the hotel, treat myself to a mini-bottle of cheap chardonnay, and sleep until I'm ready to wake up. When I rise, I am so grateful to the world, my husband, my son. Mostly I am grateful for the silence of my own thoughts and the ability to peer into them without the jarring voice of self-criticism and guilt that often runs the show.

Decide what taking some time would look like for you. What would give you a big break, and what's something you can try to do more often? Maybe it's taking a walk around the block or sitting in silence for ten minutes each day. I know it's not easy, and I have no idea what this would look like in your life if you're a single mom with three kids and three jobs. Maybe it's just deciding for one night to not pick up the eight thousand small toy pieces that give you black-and-blues on your feet every time you step on them. Perhaps one day a week you could take the free time when the kids are asleep and not pay the bills, not pack the lunch, not do laundry, not clean the kitchen, but just sit and breathe.

Whatever it is, you can't give your family what you don't have. If you're running on empty, your kids are just getting the exhaust fumes and gunk that's glommed onto the bottom of your tank. When you take time for yourself, you don't just gain physical energy, you replenish your fortitude, creativity, resilience, and capacity to love. Just what your family needs.

Thought Experiment:
Take a Break!

How often do you need a break? How often do you get one? What's the conversation that goes on in your head about whether or not to take one? Is the conversation really true? What's more important, your guilt or your sanity?

[Sanity Savers]

Here are some tips for taking care of yourself and getting what you need.

1. Visualize what taking time for yourself looks like for you. Create an image that you can escape to when you need a break and can't get one. If you can't rent a hotel room, what can you manage in an hour? A bubble bath? A manicure? A walk in nature? As mothers, we need a daily metaphoric hotel room.

Here's an idea from one very creative mom: "In the overwhelming twelve hours I'm with my kids each day, I need to do something for myself. I get them set up with something (play dough, bubbles) and ask them if there's anything else they need because once I set them up, I'm taking a solid twenty minutes and diving into a book. They have to deal with it. It's no hotel room, but it's sure been nice to see them get along without me even though I'm in the same room. I'm there, but I've checked out for a little while to soothe my sanity."

2. Write a want ad, a succinct description of what you need, and then reply to it. This will help you be clear about what you can do.

3. The serenity prayer (used by twelve-step groups) is: "God grant me the serenity to accept the things I cannot change, courage to change the things I can, and wisdom to know the difference." What are the things in your life as a mother that you cannot change? What can you change? How do you know the difference?

4. Set limits. When your cup is empty, take a break. Call on your family, friends, neighbors, and health club to get the help you need.

5. Ignore shame. When you need help, ask for it.

6. Listen to your intuition. What is it telling you right now? Awaken your inner knowing by listening to what your soul is asking for.

7. Ask your kids for help. A two-year-old can put napkins on the table, wash vegetables, pour kibble into the cat's bowl. Getting them to help is good for you and good for them.

8. Most important, do things that will lead you back to yourself rather than to more distraction and consumption.

9. Don't rush to do errands in your brief time to yourself. That's not a break, it's more work.

I'm Beginning to Ask for Help

NIKKI KATZ, 30
MOM OF KATELYN, 3, AND
KENDALL, 15 MONTHS

I'm a work-at-home mom, and even when I have an extremely tight deadline, I find it hard to ask for help. I don't want to search out others to parent instead of me. That's *my* job, and it's one I'd better excel at, I tell myself. I fear what would happen to my psyche if I got somebody to help me. What if Katelyn went to this "other woman" when she skinned her knee, instead of me? What if Kendall took her a book to read, instead of toddling into the office to climb in my lap? Honestly, it would break my heart.

I don't ever want to be accused of not being able to handle parenthood. I want to have it all—being a mommy, a wife, a writer, and a friend; keeping a nice home; and cooking a great meal. That also means being perfect at everything I do. I have this immense fear of being judged. But modern moms tend to do that. They judge their peers, their parenting styles, and their children's behavior. It's become a huge contest to see whose child can be the brightest, most talented, most beautiful, most social, most well-mannered, and most well-rounded.

I'm slowly beginning to ask for help. I feel an immense amount of guilt on the days when I'm holed up in the office with a tight deadline and the girls are running circles around the television. I feel guilty for losing my patience and my temper. I feel guilty for putting off reading a story when I need to check my e-mails one last time. So I've started off small, asking my mother-in-law to help out one afternoon a week. I know the kids are safe and having a great time. It's been going well, and I'm learning to enjoy the peace and quiet while I focus on work. In fact, I'm expanding my horizons and looking for a mother's helper to assist on another afternoon. I find that the time I spend away from my children helps in many ways. I give dedicated attention to my work for a set amount of time, and then I come home and give dedicated attention to the girls. I actually miss them when I'm working, instead of being aggravated that they are around.

· 3 ·

We're not in control
(we never have been and
we never will be)

"Do you ever feel helpless as a mother?" I cautiously asked my friend Pam.

"When don't I?" was her response. We both let out a nervous laugh—we are control freaks. In fact, the tension of feeling helpless while desperately wanting to be in control is something that sets my teeth on edge every day of my mothering life.

For instance, there's no hiding from anyone that I am a food Nazi when it comes to my child. I've read mountains of material on childhood nutrition, brain growth, omega-3 fatty acids, pesticides, mercury, sugar, hydrogenated oils, and all about how our poisoned planet is making its way into the digestive systems of our little ones. I'm a mama lion about what passes my child's lips.

For months my kitchen was splattered with pureed organic butternut squash, sweet potatoes, carrots, and peas as I laboriously made all of Zak's food. Boy, did this make me feel in control. I felt a deep sense of satisfaction (and not a small amount of self-righteousness) when I would walk through the mall and see ten-month-olds eating french fries from their stroller trays. Imagine my horror when I saw a one-year-old drinking Mountain Dew straight from the bottle.

But when I look honestly at myself, I have to admit that it's as if I've got a death grip on my child's eating habits. I feel personally assaulted when anyone, including the pediatrician, wants to cram a lollipop into his mouth. Admittedly, getting my kid to eat right is not the worst obsession in the world, but this fixation only gives me the illusion of control.

On a trip home to New York when Zak was just over one year old, I was forced to let go. My brothers took endless joy in feeding Zak pizza right in front of me. (I practiced deep breathing during this experience—pizza has some nutritional value, right?) Then, when I returned from a trip to the bathroom, I saw my sister-in-law had given Zak a little plastic cup filled with diet soda. *Diet soda!* Zak looked up at me and said, "Ummmm, jooce." My blood began to boil. Then imagine my delight when, a few moments later, I saw him toddling out of the kitchen with a chocolate chip cookie the size of his head. But surprise, surprise, the next day he was alive and feeling just fine, with no obvious ill effects from his junk food binge and no lingering obsession with Diet Coke.

It's easy to get caught up in trying to control every aspect of our kids' lives, whether it's an obsession with what they eat, what preschool they'll go to, or who their friends are when they're adolescents. Taking control as a parent is not all bad; the challenge is figuring out when to let go. No child will thrive if you allow too much freedom—that's a great way to create a spoiled brat who never learns limits. But there are bumps and scrapes and eventually decisions that our kids need to make on their own in order to grow into who they are meant to be.

Knowing when to hold on and when to let go, when to be in control and when to give in to helplessness is a hard-earned wisdom. Yet in the long run this is the master lesson of parenting. The sooner you make friends with helplessness as a parent, the longer and happier you will live.

A few years ago, I was swimming at a pond deep in the woods in Big Sur, California. I noticed a mother quietly looking on as her beautiful twelve-year-old boy scaled the side of a small cliff so that he could leap off into the water. I was almost too frightened to watch this myself, and I couldn't help asking how she could show such calm and restraint.

"I've been on my own with two boys since they were very little," she said. "You can't be there to protect them at every turn. You learn that your job is to help them understand their own limits."

Sure enough, the boy got to a certain point, realized that he couldn't make it to the top, and turned around and came back down. She flashed a knowing smile of relief.

I learned my first lesson about letting go of control when Zak got a mysterious bumpy rash when he was barely a year old. At the doctor's office, two experienced dermatologists engaged in a professional battle of "I'm right" while standing over my little guy's curly blond head.

"This is a viral rash, a reaction to a cold virus," one asserted.

"No, it's molluscum contagiosum," the other said (sentencing my son to a condition that could last for years).

"Don't do anything," said the first.

"We could burn them off with liquid nitrogen," said the other.

Hmmm . . . Burn them off with liquid nitrogen? I thought. *Come here and let me rip your head off with my bare teeth— you let me know how that feels, OK?* Liquid nitrogen, a baby? What were these guys talking about?

Zak and I stumbled out of the posh offices, clueless about what to do next. I got home and scoured the Internet, downloading images of every kind of baby rash known to humanity. Intermittently, I grabbed him and eyeballed the rash. Did it have a hollow center? Was it large and shiny? How red was it? The questions swirled, largely unanswered, as I tried to study my way into control of the situation.

Bottom line: My little boy was uncomfortable, and not only couldn't I help him, I couldn't even figure out whether he had a serious health problem. Tears waited with anticipation at the edges of my eyes. I felt completely out of control. It wasn't the first time I had felt this way, and I knew it was far from the last. I realized that as long as Zak and I inhabit the same planet, and possibly beyond, I will always struggle with this feeling. Broken toys, a broken heart, broken dreams, and a broken world—he and I will have to face all these and more in the kaleidoscope of things to come.

When I was single and the queen of my circumstances, I would have found a way to escape feeling like this. If I was confronted by something that I couldn't control in my life, like a boyfriend with whom I was quarreling or an indecisive potential client whose decision determined my financial well-being, I would anesthetize myself by keeping inordinately busy. I numbed myself by exercising, working, seeing friends, or taking refuge in the dark anonymity of a movie theater. But now there was no running away; I couldn't abandon my son by numbing out. I was face-to-face with my greatest fear: not having control.

Then a new awareness came into focus: I can't interfere with the natural processes that Zak must go through in his life. So often what seems harsh or cruel, as we're experiencing it with our children, is in reality strengthening them for the time ahead.

I'm often reminded of the story of the little boy who sees a butterfly beating its wings wildly as it tries to emerge from its cocoon. The butterfly appears as though it will die in its furious attempt to break free. Desperate to help, the little boy pushes the cocoon apart and frees the butterfly.

Although the butterfly springs out, it immediately falls to the ground and dies.

The only way that a butterfly can strengthen its wings is by beating them against the cocoon. In his attempts to help, the boy prevented the butterfly from developing the strength it would need to survive. Likewise, my job as a mother is not to keep my son free from all suffering. The greatest gift I can give him is to keep letting go each time I find myself gripping tighter so that he can learn to fly on his own.

Thought Experiment: Losing Control

Where in your parenting practice does your need to control show up? Write this down.

What do you think are absolute musts for your child, in terms of how he learns, how she eats, how he behaves, and so forth? How do you feel when you can't control these aspects of your child's life? How do you handle these feelings of helplessness? Do you force the issue, cajole your child, or step back and let things be?

What would it be like to relinquish control, even in your imagination? Does the thought fill you with relief or frighten you? How do you relinquish the need to control, the need to judge, and the need to understand?

[*Sanity Saver*]

Sheila Ellison, prolific author and creator of www .CompleteMom.com, offers a wonderful exercise to help control freaks begin to let go.

In your home there are many jobs that need to be done, and most everyone has a specific way they want the job done. Give yourself a practice week of letting go and letting others accomplish tasks their own way. Start with something simple like the way the laundry is folded, or the way the dishes are loaded. For one whole week you are not allowed to correct anyone; they simply need to get the job done. At the end of the week, notice how it feels to have let go of control. Look for other areas in your life where you could do the same thing. If you get good at this, you'll notice more time and much less stress in your day.

Embracing Helplessness

MELANIE SPIEGELMAN, 40

MOM OF JACOB, 2

Shortly after Jacob was born, I read several books about child development and parenting. All the books said that he should roll over between six and sixteen weeks of age. He was a perfect baby and I expected him to reach all of his developmental milestones easily.

At about twelve weeks, I started to get concerned. He was healthy and strong, but he showed absolutely no signs of progress toward rolling over. I thought maybe he needed some coaching, so I tried to "teach" him to roll over. Starting on his stomach, I gently rolled him on his side and let him roll over onto his back. My efforts seemed to have no effect. I was really getting concerned as his four-month birthday approached. Then out of the blue, on the day he turned sixteen weeks, he rolled over. When he was ready, he just did it. My worrying did nothing but aggravate me.

Similarly, Jacob never had an interest in crawling. Trying to learn from our rolling-over experience, I attempted not to be concerned as all his playmates crawled around him. Well-meaning friends would tell me stories about kids who didn't crawl and later had problems with coordination or even reading. I did my best not to worry. The pediatrician said Jacob was healthy and saw no reason for concern. At thirteen months Jacob started walking without ever crawling. A week later, he was running. At fourteen months he crawled. I have a son who does things in his own way, in his own time. He and I are happier embracing this and not letting my own insecurities, our friends, or especially my in-laws make us nuts!

· 4 ·

Don't forget to howl
at the moon

I'm a bitch, I'm a lover
I'm a child, I'm a mother
I'm a sinner, I'm a saint
I do not feel ashamed
I'm your hell, I'm your dream
I'm nothing in between
You know you wouldn't want it
any other way

MEREDITH BROOKS
"BITCH"

"YOU CAN PARENT young children and still have a rich creative life," my friend Stephanie said to me. "You just have to be very, very focused."

Really, I thought, reviewing in my head the several dozen times I'd been foiled in trying to get back to writing over the past year. Every mother I knew was completely overwhelmed by the billions of details in her life, and I was no exception.

A fresh story idea popped into my head one day when Zak was about thirteen months old. At the time, I was pulling out of a parking spot in downtown San Diego after running a bunch of errands with him. I knew that I needed to write down my idea or I would forget it. I dug into my bag for a pen and pulled out a crud-covered yellow crayon. I dug again and pulled out a capless, dried-out magenta marker. I finally found a pen, only to look up and see the parking enforcement officer standing on the sidewalk beside my car, poised to give me a ticket. By this time I'd forgotten my idea.

Grumbling to myself, I pulled out of the parking spot. I felt overwhelmed by all the *stuff* in my life—the constant interruptions, the multiple commitments, and the inability to reach down into my creative source for more than two minutes at a time. It's like trying to find a radio station when you're driving across the desert. You start to get a promising signal, tune in to a great oldie for a minute or two, and then static overwhelms the airwaves and you've got to drive another fifty miles before you can hope to hear another station.

It's a challenge to parent a young child and stay tuned in to ourselves at the same time. What are our deepest longings beyond loving our children? Who are we at our roots? When and how do we get back to tending our own garden, so to speak, without feeling guilty and selfish?

Sometime after my baby's first birthday, I had this awe-inspiring revelation: *I am still me. I have an identity separate from being Zak's mom.* This realization came during a birthday party for John, a client of ours. As marketing consultants, my husband and I have been fortunate to work with fascinating people. We felt privileged to be invited to this party.

John's wife was beautiful, a successful attorney. His friends were great, funny, heartfelt, and full of life. It was a beautiful summer night, warm, with a sultry breeze that kept us all comfortable on John's expansive patio over-looking a scenic valley. We sat for hours around a fire just talking, having fun, getting to know each other.

I felt a sense of freedom, as if something heavy had

lifted from my heart. I felt like I was single again—no weight of negotiating a relationship, no fear of when I'd hear the first cry of "Mama" the next morning. My mother was visiting and she had offered to take care of Zak the following morning so that we could sleep in. I breathed a sigh of relief and smiled just thinking about the extra rest that awaited me.

I felt the night air glide slowly and gently down my back, reaching around and caressing my neck, arms, and chest. I could have taken flight. Not a care in the world. I couldn't remember when I had last felt that way.

I went through so many years of being single, trying to meet the right guy. This was coupled with an intense longing for a child, someone I could nurture, someone who could receive my immense love. Even though all of my dreams have come true, there's also something of me that I've left behind. Sometimes as mothers we look up from our daily routines and feel that there has been some sort of betrayal of our most authentic selves. We ask ourselves, "Where did I go?" No matter how much we look forward to having a family, there's a conscious or unconscious renegotiating we tend to do with ourselves in order to come to terms with who we were Before Baby and who we've become After Baby.

I remember one day when I was in my midtwenties, bike riding to Gooseberry Beach in Newport, Rhode Island. It was a glorious, steamy July day. My body felt immensely powerful. The sun shimmered as the heat beat down. My perspiration was dripping, my heart was pounding, and my chest was heaving. That was me. I was in my body, in the moment, totally in love with who I was—proud of my accomplishments.

There are moments now when it's as if I see that girl shimmering on the horizon. I desperately want to reach out and touch her. And then the phone rings, or my husband annoys me, or the weight of what I'm trying to carry presses against me and the mirage evaporates.

But that young woman feels like an essential part of me. She's wild, alarming, and totally out of control. She wants to flirt, dance, travel to the most exotic crevices of the world, speak Swahili, rescue a poor little jungle baby from starvation, soothe the woes of a planet in pain.

I have met so many mothers whose wild woman flickers to life after the first three sips of a martini. Their memories, dreams, and fantasies run from their lips like a naughty little secret that they must tell. As soon as the truth escapes, it's corralled by testaments about the joys of life with children. But I always want to hear more. I want to hear about the dark stuff, the deep-down longings, the lusts, the last time they had sex on a park bench. I want to hear about their outrage at the state of the world, the fire in their belly about not letting another son or daughter be killed in an incomprehensible war. I want to know that they want one thing today and will want something different tomorrow, because within the soul of every woman lies a powerful creative force and an ageless knowing that longs for new experiences.

Not losing touch with our passionate core, with all of its imperfection, vagaries, drive, love, and feminine essence—this is the most important legacy we can leave our children. How will they learn to express themselves if we don't model it for them? How will we grow from this brain reconfiguration called parenting if we don't integrate who we were with the incredible responsibility and love that now occupies so much of our waking thoughts?

One night just before Zak's bedtime, my husband put some music on. Elvis, Elmo, and Michael Jackson crooned for us in succession. Soon the three of us were dancing like no one was watching. I closed my eyes and felt just like I did that day on Gooseberry Beach. We'd never been so entrained as a family. That night, rather than plopping in front of the television after Zak went to bed, I sat down and journaled ideas for my next book. Great big ideas—the kind I hadn't allowed myself to imagine since I became a mother—came right through me. By releasing my inhibitions and reconnecting with my body and my passion, I had allowed the creative force to roll in.

Our children can only be themselves. Until we teach them, they have no idea how to bury their needs or desires. This authenticity is the wellspring of all creativity. We can never be ourselves when we're afraid of what everyone else is thinking, or when we break ourselves in half trying to fit into what convention wants us to be.

But how can we bring who we really are to the role of parent? How can we politely decline the media's invitation to be perfect at this new responsibility and instead bring our own unique, quirky passions to this baby-raising thing?

I've always felt very connected to the pantheon of Greek goddesses and have studied their archetypes in depth. If I want to conjure up the source of my own authenticity, I summon the essences of two Greek goddesses whose archetypes are completely opposite: Aphrodite (the Romans called her Venus) and Artemis (Diana to the Romans).

I feel most creative when I feel the most connected with my body—in touch with my femininity and sexual essence.

I call it Aphrodite energy. Aphrodite is the Greek goddess of love and sexuality (think Angelina Jolie). She holds nothing back and is not ashamed of any part of her past or her desires.

Your internal Aphrodite can be awakened through dance, touch, aromatherapy, or music. Aphrodite energy can be found in your second chakra, your pelvic area. This is the source of all creative energy—in fact it's the place where you created your children. Next time you're working on something creative, whether it's painting the bathroom, gardening, or a project at work, see if you can notice heat and energy being generated from this area.

If you're feeling tired, overburdened, and angry, I guarantee you that Aphrodite wants nothing to do with these feelings and she cannot be found. (Notice how you've got no libido when you're angry and resentful at your partner for not helping with the load you're carrying.) Notice also how drained your creative force is when resentments and stress are obscuring your Aphrodite energy.

Artemis energy, on the other hand, activates very different characteristics. Artemis is the Greek goddess of the wilderness, the moon, the hunt, and wild animals. She is a warrior, often pictured armed with a bow and arrow. She roamed the mountain forests and uncultivated land, hunting wild animals. Although she was a virgin goddess, she was the goddess of fertility and protector of children and animals. Artemis didn't let any man mess with her, and if a man tried, he faced her wrath (think Hillary Clinton or Martha Stewart). For me, Artemis represents a fierce independence, a self-reliance and self-direction that also invokes my most authentic self. When nothing is standing in my way and I feel most independent and purposeful, I know that Artemis energy has been activated.

Artemis energy is that feeling you get when you've made your own decisions, pursued a goal and achieved it, and only need to look inside yourself for the right answers. No one else's opinion matters. You've hit your stride and, at least for the moment, you know in which direction you're heading.

Every woman will find in herself one or more of the Greek heroines. Knowledge of the goddesses can provide you with a way of understanding yourself and your relationships with men, women, and your own children. By summoning your internal goddess through meditation, breath work, music, and dance, you can repeatedly bring back into focus those parts of yourself that are longing for expression. But don't forget, when you're feeling most stomped on by life and need to rejuvenate your goddess energy quickly, you can choose to just step outside and, literally or metaphorically, howl at the moon.

Thought Experiment: Summoning the Goddesses

What aspects of yourself have gone into hiding since you became a mother? Can you see where in your life allowing your whole self to show up could spark your creativity?

When was the last time you felt really sexy, carefree, in your body? How can you summon that feeling again?

It's easier for us as mothers to summon Artemis energy because we're pushed to make decisions every day, but when was the last time you really let go of what other people thought? Notice your own internal judgments. Relinquish your need to be accepted by others. Feel how liberating this is, how it allows your energy to flow unobstructed.

What would happen if you unveiled your wild child, your internal goddess, to your children? (They will glimpse her anyway, whether you're howling at the moon or trying to pretend she doesn't exist.)

[Sanity Savers]

Here are some tips for getting in touch with the "you" inside.

1. Read *Goddesses in Everywoman* by Jean Shinoda Bolen.

2. Take every opportunity to dance, sing, and move your body—by yourself, with your kids, with your husband. Notice if anything inside you releases.

3. At least once a week, really take time to get dressed. Take a longer-than-usual shower, shave your legs, condition your hair for just a few minutes longer. Get out of the sweats, put on lipstick. Do whatever you need to do to feel really sexy.

4. Spend some time with people you share a passion with, people who can help you connect with the parts of yourself that are beyond being a mother.

Motherrunner

ELEEN KELLY

Before I was a mother, I was an ultrarunner. I ran marathons, then back-to-back marathons, then a 60-kilometer race, then a couple of 50-milers, then, at last, a 100K (61.2 miles). Before I had kids, I worried that my ultrarunning was a sign I was unfit to be a mother. The loneliness of the long-distance runner has nothing on the oddball misanthropy of the long-, *long*-distance runner. But I was married, and I wanted kids, so I had one, a daughter, and two years later, a son.

Mothering is, after all, an extreme sport. And I've learned from ultrarunning how to tackle a sport when I don't have a lick of talent or skill. I am that astonishing athlete who can't throw a Frisbee, catch a fly ball, complete a layup, or beat her four-year-old in a sprint to the mailbox. My sole athletic gift is the capacity to *not stop running*. I can run when I'm hungry, when I'm blistering, when I'm chafing, when I've fallen on asphalt and I'm bleeding from the knees. Of course I can be a mother; I already know how to go on when I'm psycho-sleepy. I know how to go on and on no matter how badly I have to pee. Would any mother be surprised to hear that an ultrarunner is that rare athlete whose performance often improves in middle age?

For a bone-weary, sleep-starved mom to rise extra-early for the hours of training that ultrarunning requires might strike some as perverse. Yet for me, postpartum, the sport has more allure than ever before.

There's my body. I loved my pregnant body and my nursing body, that whole full-moon-and-high-tide thing. But running, and running, I return to a sense of my body that I misplaced when I started having kids. It's not that training gives me back the abs I could spin quarters on. I don't even want *that* body back. I like the little jiggle of belly that will forever remind me of the pouch in which my babies grew. But running, *and* running, returns me to the feeling of being a body that is light-footed and tireless and strong. Running, I seem to travel in a child's body, a girl's body. Sometimes, hours later, when I'm shoving uphill a double stroller loaded with two kids and more bags than the Joads lugged to California, I'll feel that girl in me shiver with life.

At times, my desire to have no one speaking to me, looking at me or touching me can get nearly crazy. At those moments, being alone is not enough. I have to be alone and running.

To be blunt, I have to be running away. The truth is, I love to rise while it's dark and my husband and kids are sleeping, slip on my running shoes, stretch and leave. I love *indecently* that moment when I step out of my building, hit the street and start running. And running. I study the buildings I pass: brownstone, townhouse, high-rise, decaying mansion. I could have that life. That life. That life, *instead*. I put distance between me and home. I start to gather speed.

No wonder I often return to my just-waking family, two or three hours later, carrying a guilt offering of muffins and scones.

My kids seem to sense the undercurrents of my sport. When I snap the bolt to our front door, they come tumbling to greet me with frantic joy. Satisfied, my daughter grabs a hunk of cranberry scone and saunters off, scattering crumbs. I lie on the kitchen floor to stretch, and my little son throws himself across my belly. He sucks his thumb. When I lift his pajama top to tickle his skin, I feel as though I'm saying, *I'm sorry. I didn't mean it. You know I'll always come back.*

· 5 ·

Wipe spit-up, change diaper
(embracing boredom)

"CAN WE PLEASE come over and visit you and Zak?" my friend Christine asked me with a note of desperation in her voice. In the background I heard her son, Eric, repeatedly asking her a question in toddler-ese, but I couldn't understand what he was saying. "If we don't leave the house now," she continued, "I will have to sit outside on the sidewalk for another hour and watch Eric search for ants. Every time he finds one, I will have to get up, inspect it, and give it a name. I've already named fifty ants today."

I could hear her breathe a sigh of relief as I said, "Sure, come on over, we can let the kids run around in the backyard." I had to smile because I could completely empathize with her plight. The boredom brought on by the recurring chores and actions of early parenting can make it seem as though time is going backward. It feels as though the hours and minutes stretch on for days.

What many mothers don't count on when they envision the perfect maternal experience is the mind-numbing boredom that often accompanies it. The early years of motherhood are full of repetitive actions that can drive the trained intellectual mind to distraction.

But why do we have to be intellectual about the business of parenting? What if it's not all "peak experiences"? What can we learn from the direct experience of our boredom?

Many centuries ago, a Zen master said upon achieving enlightenment, "Magical power, marvelous action, chopping wood, carrying water!" This expressed the insight that when we bring our full awareness to the present moment, everyday tasks can take on a new, more meaningful quality.

For mothers raising young children, instead of "chopping wood, carrying water" it's "wiping spit-up, changing diapers." There's an elegant simplicity and profundity to the everyday experience of mothering. In fact, if we surrender to it rather than trying to change it, there's an opportunity to embrace boredom and be completely present to these simple moments that will soon be gone. But why is this so difficult?

There's a league of women in this country who, like me, spent their youth training to be successful. As we were growing up, we were told by our educators, our parents, our mentors that we could be anything that we wanted to be.

I'll never forget a teacher I had in high school, Ms. Miller. She taught a class on feminism and came to school in army fatigues, her hair a frizzy mess, looking as unfeminine as possible. She proudly wore a badge of victimhood as she told us the story of how she had been raped and that this was connected with all the violence against women in our society. Of course she was right, but there were no soft edges around her view of men. The message I got from her was: Don't even dream of selling out to the white-picket-fence dream. Go out, conquer men, kill them, vanquish them, take the spoils you deserve. In other words, take what men have by becoming a man yourself.

Of course, not everyone had Ms. Miller in eleventh grade to scare the feminine goddess into retreat for the next thirty years, but most of us who grew up in the sixties and seventies did get many messages about how important it was to succeed professionally. And so, many of us ignored the drive for family in order to have a career first.

I spent years working to get a promotion at my middle-management health-insurance marketing job. I became lean and mean, went to business school, wore the suits with the scarves that were supposed to look like ties. I tried very hard to mold myself into something that I wasn't and nearly turned myself inside out trying to do so. I was a "driver,"aggressive and determined, and used every ounce of my creativity to push my career forward.

When it came to raising a baby, I went after it as though I wanted to become CEO of motherhood. From the moment I found out I was pregnant, the classical music was flowing, I read every parenting book, and when the baby popped out, the race really got going. I pursued parenting as though I would be up for a review every six months.

The scary thing is that all the professional resources we've developed over the years—our brains, grit, ability to muscle through any obstacle the way we did in career-land—is no match for what this tiny human needs from us. This baby who steals our hearts, who scares us to death, and whom we love more than we ever thought imaginable needs something completely different from our drive and ambition. Our baby needs us to "wipe spit-up, change diaper"—to perform an endless series of repetitive tasks with our full attention and awareness.

If we let them, our children can show us the way to see the wonder in the moment, no matter how ordinary it may seem. When we're stuck in traffic, I notice Zak's eyes darting everywhere: the sky, the moon, the cars, the people, and the artwork on trucks are all objects of fascination for him. Sometimes I'll ask him what color the clouds are. My budding painter will respond, "Pink . . . yellow . . . white . . . blue . . . gray." Once again he has led me back to the richness of the moment.

Could it be that the boredom we feel isn't even boredom? We're so used to doing, plugging in, being "on," racing to be productive. Let your child show you how to *be,* even when you feel like you can't handle another minute of tedium. Get rid of the stroller and let your toddler lead you on a walk around the block. You'll be amazed at how many times she'll stop to check out small objects such as an interesting rock, a dead leaf, or an anthill. She isn't trying to drive you crazy by dawdling. To her, the journey is as exciting as the destination and the small details of the world are irresistible.

What can open up for you by rediscovering the wonder of the world through your child's eyes? This *is* the peak experience of parenting.

Thought Experiment: Surrendering to Boredom

What can we learn if we look into the face of boredom while we are raising our kids?

What is available if you are just present to your annoyance and frustration? Notice how many times you are pulled to do something other than what you are doing. Do you have to go check your e-mail one more time? Call your girlfriend to make plans? Figure out a way to get out of the house before you go stir-crazy? Listen to the chatter up there. Don't judge it, just listen.

[*Sanity Savers*]

Here are some tips for working through the boredom.

1. Find the vitality in the boring moment. Notice the details. Play off what's fascinating to your child. Let her point out all of the red trucks, blue cars, purple flowers as you drive.

2. Let the quietness of the world open up for you, even when you're not with your child. Watch slugs on the driveway, watch the clouds drift by.

3. Spend five minutes with your child turning over rocks in a park—watch the life that's going on right under your feet.

4. Observe what you are feeling when you get down on the floor and play with those Legos for the millionth time. Go a little further and allow yourself to see through your child's eyes the joy in this simple repetition. Can you just be there with your child, right in the moment, without needing it to be exciting?

5. For one day, one afternoon, one hour, stay with the boredom. Don't fight to get out of it. Notice your thoughts, notice your child noticing the world. Surrender. See what's on the other side.

The Opposite of Boredom

MARIA BERTRAND, 32
MOM OF JOSEPH, 4
AND LOIC, 2

My friend Maria has a lot to say about looking into the face of boredom when it comes to raising kids. She sent me this story about seeing what's available to her if she is just present to her annoyance and frustration.

I was having a rough day—feeling alone, sad, listless. It was that terrible three P.M. hour when naps are finished, Daddy's not going to be home for a while, and I'm beat. I sat on the sun-drenched floor of my bedroom, propped up against the ottoman of my reading chair, watching Loic scuttle around on the floor. He lunged forward from a sitting position to pick up a plastic star I'd tossed onto the carpet.

Losing interest after only seconds, he crawled quickly to my bookshelf, pulled himself up, and stretched as far as he could to the upper shelf. Then he collapsed onto his knees, onto his belly, buried his head on the floor, then looked up teasingly at me.

I thought about how bored I was, how I was tired of being a slug on the floor hour after hour, how hard this parenting gig was. I couldn't wait till the evening—I was headed to yoga with my neighbor, and that always up-lifted and rejuvenated me.

At that moment the proverbial lightbulb went on. In staring with glazed eyes at Loic's meanderings, I suddenly realized that he was moving from one yoga pose to the next: down dog, child's pose, mountain. He was lithe and aware of himself, moving half the time, it seemed to me, for the pure joy of the movement. And here I was, on the sidelines, missing it all!

It was such a revelation that I laughed, perked up immediately, and got into a pose alongside him. "Do you want to do yoga, Loic?" I asked, smiling, and he bounded over to me full of joy. The whole meaning of yoga hit me like a wave. It was this: focusing on the simplicity of movement and breathing and mindfulness so that all the love and well-being of the earth can rush right in.

• 6 •

You're right, I'm not good enough

SOCIETY HAS PERFECTED the art of telling mothers that we're not good enough. Being not good enough is good for the economy, after all. If we were already providing our children with everything they needed to be healthy, safe, and superintelligent, we wouldn't need black-and-white mobiles to stimulate their neonatal intelligence, pricey baby skin-care products to prevent irritation, or scientifically researched videos to teach our one-year-olds to read (before it's too late!).

In every toy store, every bookstore, every solicitation of my playgroup is the suggestion that somehow I'm not good enough as a mother. I saw a book the other day entitled something like *200 Math Exercises Your Child Should Do Before Two Years*. I thought of my two-year-old's counting skills: "one, three, fourteen . . ." There it is again: I'm not doing my job.

One day I was watching my nails dry at the nail salon and chatting with the mother of a three-year-old girl. When I told her that I have a two-year-old, she perked up and told me that I must put his name in to attend the Genesee School as soon as possible since the waiting list is so long. I told her that we were already attending a small preschool program a couple of days a week together and it seemed just fine. She promptly informed me that she had considered all of the preschools in the area and the one my son was attending wasn't "international" enough for her. Since there was only one other white family in our class of thirteen, I wondered what her criterion for "international" was.

She went on to inform me that the Genesee School was the most "academic" of all of the schools that she had visited and that was why she chose it. I looked at her somewhat incredulously and said, "He's two years old. I'm not sure I want to push him too hard right now."

Now it was her turn to look incredulous. "Well, I guess some mothers feel that way," was all she said.

The conversation seemed to be over. But sitting in the next pedicure seat was another mom. "You know," she said, "I sent my kid to Genesee and had him in a bunch of extracurricular classes. Now he's eight years old and completely burned out. He resists doing anything new. These days he doesn't want to get out of bed in the morning. He's had it." She went on, "If I had it to do over again, I never would have put him in such a high-pressure school. I would have kept him home to play with worms in the backyard."

Up to this point, the conversation had been pushing my "who's the better parent" button (which gets pressed ten times each day), but this mother with the burned-out kid stopped me in my tracks and taught me something I will never forget.

In today's push toward "perfect parenting," many of us are driving ourselves and our children crazy. When we follow the lead of a world gone mad, we often disregard the true nature and the real needs of our children. I realized then and there that the only thing that matters is what's right for my kid—not what everyone else thinks is right for him. And at two years old, who is it who can best understand and advocate for him? I hope it's his parents.

Next time someone makes you feel not good enough, listen to your own intuition. If someone's trying to convince you that $800 water-survival swim lessons are imperative for your six-month-old because otherwise your child could easily drown, consider your own circumstances. Maybe you'll think, *Hmmm . . . since we live in the desert and don't have a pool, I don't want to traumatize my daughter just yet.* If you think it's time to go one way and everyone else tells you to go another way, listen to yourself. Be sensitive to your own instincts and circumstances.

I myself didn't go to preschool (and look at me now, an illiterate threat to society), but I was a precocious preschooler. My mother had me reading by the time I was four years old, and I ended up completing first and second grade in one year. This contributed heaps and mounds to my self-esteem—I always knew I was smart and articulate—but I'm not certain it made me happy.

I want my son to be happy. Sure, I want him to be academically successful, but mostly so that he doesn't feel like a dope and believes that he can succeed on whatever path he chooses.

Our most important job as parents is to help our children find their bliss, to give them plenty of opportunities to discover what *they* really love and to encourage them to follow their inner voice. My deepest intuition about parenting is to give my child as many open-ended opportunities to play as possible—to let him explore and create and imagine and to uncover the wonders of the world we live in, all on his own.

But I didn't always see it this way. I filled our backyard with creative crafts projects, Little Tikes cookware, a tricycle, and more. But my son is often most happy picking up and stacking the rocks in the side yard, finding leaves, and studying anthills. He can spend fifteen minutes watching a spider spin her web.

It's painful getting sucked into feeling that I'm not good enough as a mother, as I did with this woman at the nail salon. The fire in my belly ignites and my heart beats a little faster. Should I be doing what she's doing? Should I send my son to the most expensive preschool in the state? How much ground will he be losing if I don't? What if he gets to kindergarten and is years behind all of those kids from Genesee? And then I have to take a deep breath and ask myself: What is best for my child? What does my intuition say versus what my ego is dictating?

My gut tells me that we don't have to hypereducate our kids. Children learn by osmosis—they absorb everything going on around them. That's why there's so much value, even early on, in incorporating our kids into the simple routines of daily life: doing the laundry, washing dishes, feeding the cat. But most of all, children learn from *who you are*. My most magical memories of my mother are of the times I saw her resilience, her drive to improve and educate herself, and her nonjudgmental love of who I was.

If you're being true to yourself, if you're staying in touch with your passions and are committed to those things that make you uniquely you, then much of your parenting job is already done. Whether you have an amazing green thumb, a love of exercise and nutrition, an inner drive to reach the top of the corporate ladder, or you make a point of consistently overtipping waiters, your kids are learning from how you are in the world.

More than once I had to leave my son for a few days in order to write this book. Often I would berate myself about not being there for him, not reading to him every day, or not being present for his music class. One day I came home after my longest stretch away. Zak and I hugged each other and danced a joyful little jig around the living room. Then he asked me in his fledgling toddler-speak, "You write book, Mama?" After silently thanking my husband for making sure Zak understood where I was, I breathed a sigh of relief.

Zak will never know that I'm not a "good mother" (until he enters the hormonal rage of adolescence). He will not feel neglected because I didn't teach him two hundred math exercises before he was two years old. What he will always know is that I am a writer. And he will know that if he wants to, he can be one too.

So there you have it—I'm not good enough. It's been a relief and liberation to accept that I will never live up to society's warped standards of the perfect parent. And if I can keep myself from caving in to the constant pressures that urge me to buy more, be more, do more, perhaps I will succeed in not being good enough for the rest of my life.

Thought Experiment: Who Says You're Not Good Enough?

When was the first time you didn't feel "good enough" as a mother? What caused this thought/feeling to arise? Who do you feel is judging you? How does this change your behavior?

[Sanity Savers]

Here are some tips for embracing that you're good enough.

1. Make a list of the things that are most important to *you* for your child to learn before kindergarten. They should reflect who you are, your background, what you really value. (My list includes: a love of music, introduction to a second language, compassion, and charity.) Remember this list when you feel pulled off-center by someone else's agenda.

2. Look at your list and start with yourself. Be those things that you want your child to learn. If you're not living out the items on your list, your child can't learn them.

3. Write a letter to the person who makes you feel inadequate (your mother, your father, your sibling, your child's teacher). Explain that you're being true to yourself and why they should be too. Put the letter in your drawer and read it from time to time, especially when you're feeling like you're not good enough.

4. Whenever you hear an inner voice saying that you're not doing enough for your child, stop and ask

yourself who wants to plant this thought in your head. Is someone trying to sell you something? Is someone trying to make you feel like you're not good enough so that you'll buy their product or service?

5. Read *Confessions of a Slacker Mom* by Muffy Mead-Ferro, a book that celebrates being "not good enough" by today's standards.

·7·

Healing the mommy wars

Experience is a riverbed,
Its source hidden, forever flowing:
Its entrance, the root of the world,
The Way moves within it:
Draw upon it; it will not run dry.
Heaven rescues and protects us
Through compassion.

TAO TE CHING

I DIDN'T UNDERSTAND what the Mommy Wars were until I visited with my friend Aisha one day when our sons were just five months old. Our children had been born the same week.

I met Aisha when she was a single, driven, New York video producer, as serious about her business as any woman I had ever met. While I was hell-bent on having children, she was always ambivalent about it. She didn't seem to hear "the call to nurture" the way I did. But now here she was with a baby, born almost the same day as mine.

That day, as we sat together, I gingerly asked her if she still had any projects percolating in her mind.

"I'm raising our son," she announced with a you-stupid-idiot snicker and an eye roll that left me closely examining the rim of the mug I was holding. The implication was that my working part-time at home was equivalent to leaving my little cub out in the cold for the elements to devour.

Time and again I've spoken to women who have been snubbed in the Mommy Wars—by mothers judging other mothers. When we give birth, many of us seem to get on a high horse, hoping and believing that what we're doing is best. I often wonder why we can't just support one another. Frequently, motherhood boils down to a series of not-so-obvious choices, some of which are merely choices between the lesser of two evils, some of which are downright agonizing. But it seems we're afraid to admit to each other that we have doubts about the choices we've made. Instead we reinforce them by putting down mothers who've made different choices. This strategy seems to give us some power and confidence, at least in the short term.

Our insecurities also contribute to the bad habit of comparing our kids and comparing ourselves as mothers. The seduction of comparison constantly beckons me, and a nasty voice starts in my head: "Oh, if I could just have a chance, I'd fix that baby's (sleep, eating, discipline) problems." I have a deep underlying belief, however, that women share a collective wisdom, intuition, and experience that transcends this kind of fearful chatter.

There's a curious interplay between this tendency to compare ourselves and our ability to mutually support each other that you can see in the zillion playgroups that can be found in towns and cities around the world. Whether the playgroup is planned or a spontaneous gathering in a playground on a raw and windy day, a lot of sanity has been saved when women come together to unload their stories from the trenches. These playgroups, which are often more for the moms than the kids, mimic the kind of tribal support that's been lost to us as we've become more isolated from our extended families.

I was invited to join a playgroup when Zak was just a few weeks old. At the time, I felt silly joining this gathering. All I could picture was a group of bourgeois suburban women chattering about the color of their baby's poop. But the fact was that I desperately needed to talk about Zak's poop (it's a long story, but it was pretty scary stuff in the beginning). Even more important, I felt that I didn't know what I was doing as a mother. Each day I felt like I was setting out on a long journey without a map. I had no experience, and I felt sure I was doing something terribly wrong. I had a constant sense of walking out on a skinny little rope without a net underneath me. One false move and I was going to break this baby in two. Having moved three thousand miles away from my mother, brothers, sisters-in-law, and college friends, I was so hungry for community that I decided to give the playgroup a try.

Our initial meetings were uneventful, and I had a creeping feeling that I had nothing more in common with these women than the fact that I had a baby—who creatively slept through our first couple of encounters. But desperate for a guiding light in the darkness of those first few months of motherhood, I stayed committed to our weekly meetings.

We gathered at various places around San Diego and schlepped our drooling little bundles around in identical Baby Björn carriers. I couldn't wait for us to get going on the obsessive baby-care discussions. But I discovered that these discussions often had an element of comparison and competition.

"How did you get him to sleep eight hours straight?" they'd ask me, after I just *happened* to mention it, knowing that sleep was an A-list topic.

I explained to them that in all of my obsessive reading, I learned that babies who are breast-fed don't sleep through the night as quickly as babies who are formula-fed. The biggest difference that I could see was that bottle-fed babies get their food a lot faster and the mother knows exactly how much the baby is drinking. (If the baby takes only one or two ounces and falls asleep, Mama is more likely to jiggle the baby and encourage her to take some more in order to finish off the bottle.) So I excitedly told the moms in our playgroup how I pumped breast milk every morning and then at night used that milk to coax Zak into taking a full feeding before I put him down for the night. (I had been told that morning milk is fattier than evening milk and keeps them fuller longer. I was encouraged to pump in the morning for that reason, label it "morning milk," and use it at bedtime.) If I didn't do this, Zak would nurse for three minutes at night, fall asleep on a completely empty stomach, and wake up three hours later, ravenous. On a nice full tummy, I didn't see him until five A.M. Happy baby, happy mama.

The sharing and comparing went on and on as we pumped each other for information. Here we were, a group of intelligent, educated women, many former breadwinners, who could talk of nothing but their babies. While we did give each other lots of support, an undercurrent of judgment and comparisons vibrated in the air.

"How's work?" at least one of the moms would ask me each week with a little smirk. (I was one of only two mothers in the group who worked.) I knew the question was a dig because she never bothered to wait for my reply.

There were women in the group who made me glad to be me, who made me feel like I wasn't the most crazed, obsessive-compulsive mom on the planet. One woman in particular was a marvel of preoccupation with her son. Every week she presented some agonizing question:

"Should I be feeding him pureed squash or carrots? I read somewhere, but I can't remember where, that carrots aren't as good for a baby as squash. What do you think?"

When her son got a little older and she prematurely seized the opportunity to potty train him, we got daily e-mails on the progress of the poop. I found her obsessiveness hysterically funny, but I also learned from her experience, gathering information that I later used with my potty-pooping straggler, Zak.

Finally it struck me. This wasn't just a playgroup. This was a circle of women—a powerful consortium. Each brought the wisdom of grandmothers and great-grandmothers. Each, to a greater or lesser degree, contributed to my expertise as a mother. Here we didn't need doctors' advice or to follow each and every rule in the book. We traded information, experiences, and lore and weighed them against our own experience.

Most important, this group taught me to trust my own intuition. I saw that there were as many ways to raise a child as there were children. Even with all of its oddities and competitive edge, my "women's circle" taught me how to listen to my inner voice—the one that tells us when to act, when to ask for help, when to just watch and wait. By sharing and examining every detail of this journey, I've also seen how deeply we are all connected. I've learned that if I feel something as a mother, others do too, and our collective voice and energy can be a powerful vehicle for change.

Becoming a mother has cracked my heart open in ways I never expected. Suddenly I went from worrying about my own day-to-day needs to worrying about the world's. The environment has become so much more important to me; political developments now affect me directly. The motivations of people around the world have become transparent to me as I see the deep love for their sons and daughters reflected in their hearts.

The Asian tsunami in December 2004 powerfully reinforced my newfound sense of connection and caring. In the end, the tsunami made me believe, even amid horrid death and destruction, that women really can change the world. As the death toll rose, incomprehensibly, to over 200,000, I didn't know what to do with my emotions about it. I was helpless, tied to my bourgeois lifestyle, avoiding the news so that I wouldn't feel the horror and the pain of it all.

And then there it was, inescapable. On the cover of the *New York Times*. A beautiful Indonesian woman dressed in a stunning sari. Brilliant reds and yellows wrapped around her. Her features were so delicate, her teeth broad and white. A small gold nose ring accented her simple beauty.

She was on her knees. Lying before her were at least a dozen children, some naked, some barely covered. At least five babies were my son's age. They were pudgy, well cared for, just beautiful. They were all dead. Her face was turned upward. A mixture of horror and bereavement pulled her mouth into a plaintive grimace. Her hands were clenched by her head in a gesture of anger and powerlessness. I brought the paper home, laid it on my coffee table, and stared at this picture on and off for nearly an hour. My heart went swirling into hers. I felt as if I had lived every moment of the birth of her children, the care, the laughter, the concern, the feedings, the changings, the frustration, the day-to-day concerns of raising children.

How could she possibly live through this pain? How have the millions of mothers who've lost children lived through their pain? Just because these people lived thousands of miles away from me, and much closer to the edge of survival, didn't make their hearts, their love, their pride any more manageable.

I had purchased the paper thinking that it was such a historic headline that I should save it and perhaps sell it on eBay in twenty years. But I quickly realized that this was more than a collector's item. It represented pain that was so immense I could barely conceive of it—and it was uncomfortably close to home. I stuffed the paper in my garbage can and closed the lid, feeling as though I was saying goodbye to that poor mother, whose grief was too much for me to bear. How simple for me. But deep down I knew that I was a breath away from her experience.

I struggled with these feelings of connection. So what if I feel connected, so what if I feel helpless? Why indulge these feelings if I'm not going to do anything about them? And then I got the e-mail. Someone in my mothers' circle had forwarded an e-mail to me from another mother, who had received it from another. It was clear that the e-mail had already gone to thousands of mothers in my community. It announced a local fund-raiser for victims of the Asian tsunami. The headline read: LOCAL MOMS HAVE SCHEDULED A ONE-DAY CASH AND CARRY SALE IN AN EFFORT TO RAISE MONEY TO AID IN SOUTHERN ASIA RELIEF EFFORTS.

What struck me the most, however, was the copy in the press release. One mother wrote, "As a mother, when I saw the images of parents grieving for their missing children and children separated from their parents or orphaned by the tsunami, I just felt an overwhelming need to do something more than write a check to help the victims of this tragedy. When I e-mailed other moms, I realized many women were feeling the same way and we decided to put together the 'Moms on a Mission' sale."

For once, rather than comparing ourselves to one another, we were caught up in something positive and truly important. This was feminine power at its best. The sense of community, proactivity, of women working for women was like a powerful elixir that healed our disease of competition and comparison. The fund-raiser was very successful. But perhaps more important, it brought together a community of women who were willing to step out of their day-to-day concerns and mobilize to open hearts and make a difference.

Then it dawned on me: Why not feel the same compassion for the neurotic woman in my playgroup as I did for the heartbreaking icon of grief thousands of miles away? I still have a tendency to jump to judgment, but at least now I am aware of that, and I'm aware that I can make another choice. I can always remember that all mothers share the same hopes and fears.

The greatest gift of this experience has been a foolproof strategy for surviving the Mommy Wars. After much mental anguish I have, for the most part, given up caring what anyone else thinks of me, and this in turn has allowed me to embrace the choices that other parents make.

I don't care if people think I shouldn't be working or if they think I should be working more. I don't care if people think I should have my kid in preschool full-time or if they think I shouldn't have him in preschool at all. I don't care if people think I am doing too many activities with my kid or too few. I don't care if his teachers think I hover over him too much or if they think I'm not attentive enough.

I have stopped looking outside myself for the right thing to do.

Raising a child is a curvy road, full of twists, turns, misleading signs, breakdowns, and times to stop to take a rest or look at the map. Your route needs to take into account the unique personality of your kid, the needs of your relationship, and your personal goals and missions.

The miracle is that once you (mostly) give up caring what anyone else thinks of your choices, you gain a remarkable ability to respect the choices that other women make. Moreover, you can feel immense compassion for the difficulty of these choices. We all want to do the right thing for our children and are terrified that we're not. The journey from comparison to compassion requires acknowledging our human frailty and undoing many of the lessons we've learned about pleasing or impressing others.

As parents, we're not perfect. We do the best we can as we come to realize that there is no "right thing." Once we can embrace this, we can embrace every other mother's struggle and gain the power of compassion.

Thought Experiment: Healing the Mommy Wars

If you feel yourself getting hot and bothered when someone asks you a pointed question about how you're raising your child (such as, "Why doesn't your husband let you stop working so that you can stay home with your family?") the topic is probably an internal battle for you, something you are feeling insecure about. What kinds of questions make you feel defensive? Why? Where do the feelings of inadequacy come from?

Is there someone in particular whom you judge or compare yourself to? What power does this give you? What does it feel like? See if you can liberate yourself from this internal dialogue.

[Sanity Savers]

Here are some tips to help you work with feeling judged.

1. When you feel inadequate or insecure as a mother, journal about it. This will help you immeasurably in resolving feelings of being "less than."

2. Look at a mom whom you've felt judged by and choose to see her a different way. Probably she just wants to feel as though she's doing the right thing. What would shift for you if you stopped feeling judged and instead felt sympathy for her situation? She too has doubts and insecurities that are coming out as judgments. Find something about this mother that you would like to emulate. Allow her to silently "mentor" you. We close ourselves off from learning and growing if we're always comparing ourselves.

3. When you feel judged, try this breathing exercise: Breathing in: "I am feeling judged." Breathing out: "I let go of judgment."

· 8 ·

Doing nothing is something worth doing

The greatest calamity is not knowing
sufficiency, no greater calamity
than desire for gain.

TAO TE CHING

I WAS IN YOGA CLASS at seven o'clock on a Tuesday morning, sitting in meditation. The yoga instructor always made some profound little statement that would stick in my brain for the rest of the day. I was anxious to hear today's theme.

On this particular morning, he pointed to the excesses of our lives, the rush to go, go, go. Do, do, do. He finally said, "My guru used to say, 'Doing nothing is something worth doing.'"

Aha, I thought, *there it is. My mantra for the day.* As soon as the class ended, my brain started "doing," and I repeated the phrase over and over in my head, hoping that I wouldn't forget it before I got to my car and could write it down.

I knew immediately that this would be an important teaching in my life as a mother, but I didn't comprehend the depth of the lesson at first. I thought he was telling me, "Slow down, bask in the moment, take a day off. Connect with the universe." That kind of thing.

Over time I saw a different meaning in his words. I noticed how driven I was to create a perfect life for my child, how I and many other mothers I know tend to overdo it with too many activities, too many toys, even too much attention and protectiveness.

By overdoing for our kids, we end up robbing them of the opportunity to develop their own creativity and resourcefulness, the ability to figure things out for themselves—and ultimately we weaken their ability to separate from us and form their own identities. Not only that, by overdoing things and overindulging our kids, we rob ourselves of perspective.

As women and mothers, we perform in a three-ring circus every day. Precariously we balance children, relationships, nourishment, education, and work along with keeping a home and so much more. It's as if we're carrying all these things across a tightrope, with the ever-present fear that something will fall off and shatter on the ground.

More often than not, what lies in pieces on the ground is our own inner peace. Our lives of plenty and "more, more, more" lead to an inner fragmentation, a breakdown of the soul. How can we achieve a state of grace and serenity amid the distraction and consumption that have become our "birthright"? How can we remain balanced, no matter what threatens to pull us off center on a day-to-day basis? There are many ways to do this, involving many disciplines, but one is perhaps most available to us: simplify. Eliminate stuff. Make a commitment to "nondoing," setting limits, not indulging our child's every desire, teaching him the value of not overdoing.

This is easy to say, yet how difficult it is to step back from our culture's overconsumption and overindulgence. It requires constant discipline to tune out the many messages, both overt and veiled, that tell us that being a good parent means providing our children with every opportunity available and indulging their every whim.

I observed the machinations of one mother in my son's Mommy & Me preschool class, a class that I felt compelled to "do." Her three-year-old son was obviously brilliant. He spoke more than other kids, knew the words to a couple of dozen songs, and had a really active imagination.

As we sat in a circle one day, the teacher read the kids *The Very Hungry Caterpillar.* This little boy, while sitting in his mom's lap, reached around, grabbed her hand, and started sucking *her* thumb. At first I didn't think anything of it and actually found it kind of cute. She explained to us that she *never* let her son cry and that this was how she found it best to soothe him. Unfortunately, he had gotten so addicted to the behavior that he wouldn't let her out of his sight. At three years of age, he didn't have a clue about how to soothe himself. Their attachment to each other became more and more challenging in the classroom as the year wore on. She jumped at every demand he made, and there were many. There was nothing she wouldn't do for him, including giving him candy, lollipops, and bubble gum to calm him down. She was clearly agitated, embarrassed, and anxious about the situation. She kept explaining to us that she tried to break him of the habit of sucking her thumb, but she just couldn't.

I know a little something myself about overdoing it as a mother in a different way. In preparation for Zak's second birthday party, I spent a week trying to get the house in perfect condition and stressing about every scratch on the furniture. The day of the party, I ran all around town in ninety-five-degree heat looking for a patio umbrella that would shade our guests from the blistering sun. I planted annuals in as many flowerpots as I could find. I got anyone with a free hand to scrub down the patio chairs for the third time in a week.

Elmo was coming and a music class was planned. Nearly fifty people were invited, including twenty children under the age of three. As the guests started arriving, Zak began to cry.

"No shoes," he wailed hysterically as I tried to put on his shoes. Then he bit me, really hard. We both cried. Zak spent his entire party shoeless and was thoroughly uninterested in the six-foot Elmo who showed up. He was only minimally interested in the music class. At least he was finally starting to get the idea about birthday cake.

By the end of the party, I hadn't talked to any of my friends. My house and my nice, clean patio furniture were a mess, and nearly half the kids left without the goody bags that I had labored over for three days.

Several months later Zak and I were invited, at the last minute, to a two-year-old's birthday party. No gifts were allowed. The party was at a little playground around the corner from me. The father showed up at the park with a Frisbee, a ball, and a cooler full of juice and cheese and crackers. The mom showed up forty minutes later with a homemade cake and the birthday girl, who chose to nap through the first half of her party. There were six adults and three kids. No goody bags, no Elmo, no three-ring circus.

The kids had a blast and ran around the park playing. The adults all got a chance to chat. No one was overwhelmed. Their house was not a mess, and everyone put on party hats and gathered around to watch Hannah blow out the candles on her birthday cake.

It reminded me of my birthday parties when I was a little girl. I just needed a little extra attention, a homemade cake, and a special dress to feel like it was a good birthday. I loved that my mother was there and that she knelt down to help me blow out the candles on the cake we had made together.

When did we parents start to think that we should substitute doing a lot of things (and buying a lot of things) for paying attention? And these days, we also seem to confuse indulgence with love. Disciplining and saying no to our children seems the equivalent of abandonment.

I wonder what this constant hum of consumption and activity does to our children's souls. I grew up knowing that I couldn't have very much. I distinctly remember wearing the same pair of tights to school every day for a month. The holes had to extend below my knees before my parents would replace them. At two dollars a pair, a selection of tights was more than my parents could afford. This "deprivation" hardwired me to be resourceful. I stop at nothing to figure out how to make do with what I have, and I love the creativity and challenge that this requires. I know that if I overdo it for my kid, I will rob him of learning this lifelong skill.

With this commitment to not overdoing or over-indulging, I've noticed a rather peculiar thing: My son actually waits for me to discipline him. Only once have I had to pick Zak up and leave a store because he "had" to have something and I wouldn't give in. With him kicking and screaming, we went to the car and I waited until he calmed down. I explained to him that each time he cried like that in a store, we would leave. I was serious. With him still whining in the backseat, I drove home.

To my amazement, he now knows that most things in stores are to look at, not to buy. If he starts to whine about something he "has" to have, all he needs is a warning and he drops the tantrum, midcry.

My life is so much simpler as a result of not giving in to him. I can see his pride in himself grow as he develops self-control. Moreover, I can see that he really loves and respects us because he feels protected by the boundaries we give him.

Disciplining Zak has taught me something about disciplining myself and controlling my urges to overdo things. It has helped me to simplify my life and to challenge myself with how little I can make do with.

And the opportunities to overdo seem endless. Over a three-month period, Zak was invited to ten birthday parties. Our preschool had a full-blown campaign under way to get us to sell chocolate to raise money for the school (I thought the tuition we paid was enough of a fund-raiser). Halloween, Hanukkah, and Christmas came and went with all of the frenetic activities that center around these holidays. After going to the little birthday party in the playground, I decided that "doing nothing is something worth doing." Now each time I am presented with a new option (read: distraction) I ask myself: Is this necessary? Will this complicate my life or simplify it?

I creatively turned down invitations to five of the ten birthday parties (two years old, my son had only one best friend and didn't need to eat birthday cake more than twice a month). I ignored the invitation to sell chocolate for the school. He can do it himself when he gets older.

I don't like decorating the house for the holidays. I don't find it fun. This year, I didn't beat myself up about it or worry about how the rest of the neighborhood viewed my mothering skills. (Was it Martha Stewart who made decorating and good parenting synonymous, or was it just me who made that connection?) At Halloween I put a couple of pumpkins outside the house and left it at that.

I reserve the right to overdo it in the future and then remind myself why I gave up the habit: I want a simpler life. I want to keep my soul intact. I want my son to have a sane life.

Already there are constant excesses that beckon our children. These will become even more burdensome as years go by. Already they most likely have too much. By pruning the excess in your life, perhaps your children will learn not to obscure the needs of their souls with the relentless pursuit of material wealth.

Search for ways to strip the excess from your life. There will always be an internal fear and questioning about whether you're achieving the right balance between giving too little and having too much. There is, however, an extraordinary freedom and inner peace in shedding burdensome activities and "things" from your life. I bet you'll quickly find that "doing nothing is something worth doing."

Thought Experiment:
An Exercise in Simplifying

For just one day, take a mental inventory of your life: How overwhelmed are you by everything you're balancing? What *must* you do, and what are you doing because you think you're supposed to? Who determines what you're "supposed" to do? How little can you get along with? How little can your child get along with?

When faced with the next opportunity to buy or do something, ask yourself: Will this bring more serenity and peace of mind into my life or more fragmentation?

[Sanity Savers]

Here are some tips for simplifying your life.

1. Read *Gift from the Sea* by Anne Morrow Lindbergh. This beautiful book contains, among other things, penetrating reflections on the demands of modern life and the importance of finding balance and nurturing one's spirit. Written in 1955, it reads as if it were written yesterday.

2. Listen to *Shepherd Moons* by Enya. The music and lyrics magically communicate the power of nature to move, to touch, to inspire awe. The ethereal quality of her voice is immediately calming and centering—listening to it leaves me connected to the larger themes of life: compassion, love, forgiveness, creativity. I suggest listening to this album on a long drive, even with your kids, and *then* thinking about what's worth "not doing."

3. Allow your children to have quiet time alone with their own imagination. Give them a bucket of sand, some cups, and a pail of water and park them on a grassy patch. Don't worry about their clothes, the grass, or the mess. Just observe what they do, how

long they can play, what they look for to help with their task. Don't be in a rush to entertain them. Let them find their own entertainment.

4. Journal about what you can get along without. Pinpoint three things you can shed, for example:

- An overly elaborate birthday party. (Who are you really doing it for, anyway?) Dare to be different: keep it simple. Save your money and your sanity.
- Buying too much. What about not purchasing the toy with the two hundred removable parts that *you* will have to pick up over the next two years.

5. Eliminate or limit contact with acquaintances with whom you can't be completely honest. It's grueling to be insincere.

Have a garage sale, or take all of the excess in your life to Goodwill. Owning too much stuff suffocates the soul. Donating what you don't really need takes all this a step further by purging your guilt as well as emptying your closets.

Slowing Down

HEATHER ROBERT, 32
MOM OF BELLA, 3

I can't stop myself from multitasking. The last time I re-member being able to focus on just one thing at a time was back when I used to smoke a lot of pot. But then I got married, gained two stepchildren, and added one of my own shortly thereafter. Now, as the mother of three, my days of single-minded concentration, drug-induced or not, are over.

I must multitask. *I must get things done*, I tell myself. Cooking dinner, I make phone calls while I chop and slice, and read magazine articles as I stir and sauté. When I'm stopped at a traffic light, I make lists of things to do; if I'm on the freeway and can't write, I record my lists into a handheld tape recorder. Even when I'm doing yoga I listen to music.

But I relish the early morning feedings with my daughter. It's three A.M. No television. No radio. No electronic toys. No voices. Just the simple sounds of the night. My baby sucking and slurping at my breast. My husband snoring softly next to me. My own breathing, slow, deep, and steady. No books. No magazines. No pens. No paper. No lists. Just my baby's hair, damp with sweat in the crook of my arm. My baby's feet, one wearing a tiny bootie, the other one without. My baby's round belly pressing against my own. Her miniature hand gripping my finger. No reading light, no bathroom light. No light but that from the moon, illuminating my baby's face. Her eyes stare into mine, full of concentration and contentment, focused on this single moment. Precise and pure. Precious and perfect.

Back to Basics *and* Balance

CATE PIETRO SMITH, 40

MOM OF EMMA, 11 MONTHS

My friend Cate is a life coach. Rather than just talking about wanting to preserve balance in her life, she used her life coaching skills to stay sane while raising her baby, Emma. Cate developed the following plan when Emma was just three months old—"the height of hell," as I call it. What a novel concept to actually plan for a sane life. I've learned a lot from Cate's program, especially the part about planning the week's menu a week in advance (that's already saved us a couple of dozen last-minute, expensive, fattening evenings eating out). Of course, flexibility is the key with any plan, especially when it comes to kids. But a plan to focus on what's important, eliminate distractions, preserve sanity, and be present to what is—now that's worth scheduling in!

To create a balanced life, I regularly ask myself a series of key questions. Here they are, with my answers filled in as examples.

What are the most important things I need right now?

1. To be present and in the moment daily
2. A household management routine that's realistic
3. Quality time with my family and friends

What will I do to get there?

To be present and in the moment daily I will:

- Breathe deeply while I'm nursing Emma and pumping
- Write twice a week for twenty minutes
- Have a heart-to-heart talk with Drew twice a week after dinner
- Do yoga or Pilates twice a week at home with DVD or in a class
- Take a long walk four times a week

To manage the household I will:

- Write the weekly menu once a week
- Grocery shop once a week
- Have dinner at home that we prepare at least five times a week
- Do laundry twice a week

- Get my car washed once a week
- Do one extra household project a month (e.g., clean and condition leather chair, move maternity clothes to garage and bring in the regular ones that fit)

To have family and friend time I will:
- Meet a friend for coffee or lunch twice a month
- E-mail one friend a week with whom I haven't been in touch for a while
- Go on a date with Drew twice a month
- Eat dinner at the dining room table nightly
- Play goofy with Emma daily

When will I do these things?
- On Fridays, I will write my menu and grocery shop for the following week
- On Sundays, I will map out the coming week with the above activities
- Every evening, I will look at how the day went and will make adjustments for the following day

What am I committed to not compromising?

- Family time
- Exercise
- Getting myself grounded and centered daily (the most important goal of all!)

• 9 •

Children are quick to forgive—are you?

Through the Tao the seeker finds,
The guilty are forgiven.

TAO TE CHING

DO YOU DREAD when the time changes in the fall and the spring? No one consulted mothers of young children about changing the clock twice a year. I particularly dread the fall time change, when the clocks move back and we gain an hour. The circadian rhythms of young children, especially babies, are not easily tampered with. If you put a baby to bed an hour later than usual, she will wake up at exactly the same time she did the morning before. She doesn't know how to tell time, so too bad for you that you have to get up with a baby at what is now 5:30 A.M., which she thinks is still 6:30 A.M.

I'm very committed to my sleep, so this is a particularly troubling time of the year for me. The first year my son and I went through it was the most traumatic, but I learned an unexpected lesson from the experience.

As usual, in late October, right before Halloween, the clocks changed back to Standard Time. Zak, who was then four months old and pretty much sleeping through the night, had trouble readjusting his internal clock to go to sleep an hour later and wake up an hour later. He did well at falling asleep at the new time but could not get the hang of sleeping an hour later. After waking up at 8:30 A.M. for almost a month, he now awoke at 6:00 A.M. with the sun streaming through a window that just a few days before had been dark at the same time. Knowing he was still exhausted, as evidenced by the fact that he kept falling asleep during his morning feeding, I put him back down to sleep.

He cried and cried. We had gone through the same nightmare a month before when I tried to get him to sleep at night. If I went back in to pick him up and comfort him, he'd be soothed until I put him back down. If I just stroked him without picking him up, he would become even more infuriated. If I put him in bed with me, he just played. Within ten minutes he'd be cranky and exhausted and would end up crying himself to sleep.

Listening to him scream, I was torn by indecision. *Three minutes,* I told myself as I watched the digits click by on my alarm clock. When three minutes passed, I agonized about how wise it was to go in now that this much time had passed. Would I be sending the wrong message, letting him know that if he cried just enough, I would come? Or was I damaging his sense of security by leaving him alone to soothe himself? (I know there is a raging debate about this, so notice what's coming up for you as you read this.)

Finally, just as I was about to go to him, I saw on our video monitor that he had fallen asleep. I could literally feel the tension drain from my body as I saw his little head rest on the mattress as he submitted to sleep. I guess the cortisol production in my brain stopped, and I breathed a huge sigh of relief. But enough stress hormones had infiltrated my body so that I felt sick to my stomach and continued to rage inwardly about the whole process.

Ninety minutes later when Zak woke up, I raced upstairs. I imagined that he would be so angry with me, so withdrawn, that he wouldn't communicate. I anticipated that he would feel too insecure to show me any love and affection because he would fear being rejected and vulnerable again.

When he greeted me with a huge smile and a series of coos and giggles, I felt as if the door to my heart had sprung open, bathing us both in pure love. His eyes were a little puffy and his chin a little red from the drool of a good cry, but his demeanor bore no trace of ill will or hurt feelings.

We went on to have a lovely day. The next morning I scooped him up from his crib and played with him in Mommy and Daddy's big bed until he fell asleep an hour later. The next morning he was back to his usual routine, completely adjusted to the time change. His inability to be angry at me allowed me to open up to a series of solutions that were motivated by love rather than fear of weakening our connection.

The experience made me think of how often I've held a grudge. If I perceived someone had done me wrong, I could hold on to it for years. In fact I was somewhat known for this, and I am sure that at one point my coworkers avoided me rather than risk insulting me. And who was I really hurting with my inability to let go? I got to feel self-righteous and indignant, while my "enemy" would feel defensive, guilty, and spiteful. This could spawn years of nasty feelings and limited possibilities between us.

Our children's lessons on forgiving and forgetting could map a whole new peace plan for the Middle East or Northern Ireland, in fact for the whole spectrum of human aggression. Maybe a baby's only choice is to love. It's only once he becomes aware that he is vulnerable and often powerless that he'll protect himself by using anger as a shield.

The fact is that babies don't just forgive, they release. They do it effortlessly. They haven't learned the ego dance that comes with needing to hold on to convince someone else of their point of view.

I started to wonder: What if I could just let go of painful feelings on the spot? What if I could just choose to let go of emotional pain by heeding Zak's lesson on releasing? We all make a choice when we decide to hold on to "being right." But who are we really hurting? What underlying emotional issue keeps popping to the surface that's holding us back from just breathing in the simple "letting go" that's available every moment?

Watch babies in a playgroup. A baby will get mad when another baby takes one of her toys. The baby may even have a tantrum. But then, in the blink of an eye, the baby comes back to play with the same friend who took the toy. She never even thinks about it again, or thinks that her friend was malicious for taking the toy. That's our own projection.

As parents of very small children, we spend immeasurable amounts of time wringing our hands, feeling guilty about all the things we haven't done right, about not following every mandate of the "attachment parenting" doctrine, and so on. Yet I have never met a baby who knew how to hold a grudge. My son's inability to be angry at me for not picking him up the very first second he started to cry, or his desire to play with a little girl who just hit him over the head with a guitar, has opened me up to a series of solutions that are motivated by love and living in the moment.

Thought Experiment:
Forgive and Forget

What grievances are you holding on to? What does this cost you in your life?

What have you done in your life that you most regret? Can you forgive yourself?

Is holding on and not forgiving sabotaging you and your family? While you are holding a grudge, who holds the power? Take back your power.

[*Sanity Savers*]

Here are some tips to help you let go of old grudges.

1. Write a letter to someone whom you cannot forgive. Explain why you're angry, why you are holding a grudge. Tell the person what you need him or her to say to you in order for you to forgive. Be specific. Imagine the person telling you what you need to hear, over and over. Destroy the letter.

2. Read *The Seven Spiritual Laws of Success* by Deepak Chopra, especially chapter 6, "The Law of Detachment."

Seeing Forgiveness
in the Mirror

PAM HENDRICKSON, 36
MOM OF JONATHAN, 2, AND
BENJAMIN, ONE MONTH

We were looking forward to a nice dinner at our friends' house where our two-year-old sons could play and we could enjoy some adult conversation and companionship. I knew for a couple of days that a fight was brewing between my husband and me, and sure enough, I chose for my time of attack ten minutes before we were supposed to leave to visit our friends. It was the night before Easter and my son's Easter basket was nowhere to be found. A tragedy of epic proportions!

To make matters worse, while my husband was away, I pulled apart the entire garage closet, ignoring my six-months-pregnant belly and my husband's promise to find the basket for me. By the time he returned and announced it was time to leave for our friends', I had worked myself into a frenzy. I launched the first salvo and a screaming match commenced. After about five minutes of yelling, I realized our son was standing there, so I scooped him up, not very gently, and put him in the house. Then I returned to the garage for round two. After five more minutes, we'd both had enough, so I stepped back into the house to look for my son.

My sweet boy stood in the middle of the kitchen floor, not having moved from where I had placed him. With his tearful eyes as big as saucers, he looked up at me. In that moment, my heart sank. *What have I done to my child? How will he ever forgive me? What kind of mother loses it like this in front of her two-year-old?*

I immediately picked him up and explained to him the philosophical intricacies of why mommies and daddies fight and, most important, that you can fight with someone and still love them very much. By the end, he was squirming about, looking for an escape route from his obviously psychotic mother. Finally, my smart little boy looked up and said, "Mommy, Daddy, fight. OK now." Then, he ran out to get in the car to go see his best friend.

I am still looking for the permanent psychological damage I have done to my son, but there are no signs of it. He had forgotten the whole thing in less than five minutes. Now it was my turn to forgive myself. I realize that it was my own inability to trust, have faith, and release that led me to unleash on my husband. It was my incessant worry that I am not good enough, strong enough, or worthy enough to deserve this incredible gift of family and love that caused me to betray my higher aspirations and behave like that.

One of the greatest gifts of motherhood is that it unveils the most profound truths in life: My lack of compassion for *myself* causes me to feel intolerant of others. The most powerful thing I can do, the best thing I can do for my family, is to forgive myself for not being perfect, for being only human. It is not about seeking forgiveness from others; it's about forgiving myself.

It's never too late to have a happy childhood

> In the beginner's mind there
> are many possibilities, in the
> expert's there are few.
>
> SHUNRYU SUZUKI
> *ZEN MIND, BEGINNER'S MIND*

THIS PAST HOLIDAY season, my in-laws did something great for me. They decided to have Christmas before Christmas, just to make it easier for us to celebrate the holiday with them. We were already traveling to Minnesota, where my husband is from, in early December.

They offered to celebrate Christmas then, rather than on the twenty-fifth.

This Christmas thing always stirs me up. I'm the daughter of Holocaust survivors. I grew up on the Upper West Side of Manhattan. I never had a Christmas tree. I never met any of my grandparents, aunts, or uncles. If they weren't killed in concentration camps, they were killed by grief. I have one first cousin, who lives seven thousand miles away from me. I met him once, when he was already a middle-aged man.

By contrast, my husband comes from a huge family. He has three siblings and nearly fifty first cousins. All told, Zak has thirteen first cousins, with more on the way. When we talk about second cousins, I'm sure *he's* got nearly fifty of them by now.

I used to feel like an odd duck in my husband's family. Minnesota and New York seemed to have vast oceans and jungles between them when I would sit in my in-laws' living room.

But then there was Christmas this year, and as ten of Zak's first cousins streamed through the door and immediately enveloped my little boy in their big, loving, playful fray, I suddenly belonged. I couldn't believe how sweet this brood was.

"My cousin, my cousin!" the littlest one screamed as she came running through the door. "I want to see my cousin!"

They picked him up, they swung him around, they showed him how to play their violin, they even sang Christmas carols to him while he banged on the piano keys. They took his hand and showed him where all of the toys were hidden in Grandma's house, and they just loved him up.

I could feel the rings around my brain peel away. As I sat there watching them roll pool balls around on the top of the pool table with complete concentration and joy, a huge sense of well-being started sizzling inside me. All the judgments, the constant, ongoing babble in my head about how things should be, about how I can't let go of my no-Christmas thing "because what would my family think?" just started a big glacier melt in my head, revealing incredible gratitude for all the love this huge family was showing me and, most important, my little guy, who seems destined to be an only child.

But the most amazing thing was that these kids had no judgment of each other. They didn't stop and inquire about where they each lived, how much money their families had, what their education was, or, most of all, what religion they were.

They just jumped in and played with each other. Everyone was welcome to join in. The games started and stopped spontaneously. One second it was hide-and-seek. The next it was playing with blocks, and then it was running up and down the stairs. There were no conditions for play, no rules, no preparation, just spontaneity.

By meeting our children where they are, not where we want them to be, we can see life with fresh new eyes again. The Buddhists call it "beginner's mind." Beginner's mind is the mind that is innocent of preconceptions and expectations, judgments and prejudices—the mind that is just present to explore and observe and see things as they are. Beginner's mind is like the mind of a small child, full of curiosity and wonder and amazement. A child doesn't approach things with a fixed point of view or a prior judgment. "What's dis?" is my son's most common question. He just needs to know for the sake of knowing.

Blanche Hartman, the abbess of the San Francisco Zen Center, asks:

Can we look at all of the aspects of our lives with this mind, just open to see what there is to see? Children begin to lose that innocent quality after a while, and soon they want to be "the one who knows." We all want to be the one who knows. But if we decide we "know" something, we are not open to other possibilities anymore. And that's a shame. We lose something very vital in our life when it's more important to us to be "one who knows" than it is to be awake to what's happening.

From watching my son, I've learned that it's never too late to have a happy childhood. You can do this by accessing your beginner's mind. Your children will show you how. This time of your life is ephemeral. Soon enough your children will grow up and you won't be able to lie naked on a beanbag chair with them and read five books as the sun streams through the windows.

So starting today, drop your inhibitions. Jump into motherhood fully. Sometimes this will mean making a mess: playing with water and mud, swinging and sliding or just staying at home and being too engaged to get out of your pajamas. Involve your children in your own sense of play, too, whether it's cooking, music, or gardening. This is pure joy.

Conclusion

Teaching without words,
benefits without actions—
few in the world can grasp it.

TAO TE CHING

I HAD BEEN MEANING to get Zak a cat for nearly a
year. There was always one excuse or another: He wasn't
big enough, we were going to be traveling too much, I
didn't want my furniture used as a scratching post.

Finally one day, when he was about two and a half, I
took him to visit a nearby animal shelter. He seemed to understand exactly what was happening as we got acquainted

with all the cats, in search of the one that would be right for us. He seemed to try each one out, getting down on the floor to be at eye level with them, gently saying hello and patting their bellies. He insisted that I tell him the name of each cat he petted and took special care to address them by name. After he found a feather "cat teaser," he dangled it in front of each cat's face, trying desperately to entertain them. If they seemed particularly uninterested in him, he wasn't dissuaded; he just kept talking to them, certain that they understood English.

When we finally came upon "the right cat," the one who curled up in Zak's lap and purred contentedly, he gingerly stroked and held it according to my hovering instructions. His eyes were full of compassion as he noted the little scab on the kitten's forehead. "What's dis?" he asked with concern.

We left that day without the kitten, but my husband picked it up the next day while Zak was napping. When he awoke and spied the kitty peeking out from behind some bedding, he got down on his knees to make eye contact. In a moment of seemingly scripted cuteness, the kitten leapt from behind the covers as if to say, "Here I am, let's play!"

Zak looked at me and shrieked with delight, "Zak's ditty-tat!" They tumbled and played as I watched, thoroughly amazed at Zak's gentleness and consideration toward this little critter. About ten minutes into it, he stopped, gently stroked the kitten's head, gave it a kiss and said, "I wuv you."

It took my breath away. In that moment, I knew that for all of the mistakes I had made as a parent (and would make in the future), I had done something right. I knew that I had taught my boy how to love. He wasn't just reiterating the words that we always said to him. It was clear that he felt and understood what it is to love.

Often when Zak cries, whether from hurting himself or not getting his way, he looks deeply into my eyes to see my love and compassion for him. I marvel at his intense scrutiny of me at these times. Now I know that I have communicated something much more powerful and succinct than words. In the same way that he emulates me screaming at the driver who cut me off, he has learned to emulate the kindness and compassion that come from the purest center of my heart.

In that moment, I understood the true work of motherhood. This was larger than me, and yet I was the vehicle. I thought of Michelangelo's painting on the ceiling of the Sistine Chapel, of God reaching out to infuse Adam's limp hand with the energy that will bring him to life. A source much bigger than me had reached through me to ignite the essence of humanity that lay in Zak's heart. What more could a mother ask for?

The hardest, most important parts of parenting are being done for you. You are not alone; your child comes equipped with the software to receive the information that she needs to grow into who she is intended to be. You just need to be present, observe, be yourself, and, most important, take care of yourself. All that you need to do is already done. Let it unfold.

Acknowledgments

LOVE AND THANKS to all of the mothers around the world who love their children enough to persevere, no matter the obstacles—my heart travels with you every day. A multitude of thanks to: my friend, comrade, and agent, Lynn Franklin, who has encouraged my growth throughout the years; Eden Steinberg, the best editor in the world—thank you for your patience and perseverance—you are a gem; all of the team at Shambhala Publications for your willingness to process all of the possibilities regarding this book—it's a pleasure to work with such mindful professionals. A million thanks to: Larisa Getmanets, my friend, my sister, and surrogate daughter, you make my life possible—I love you; Pam, Chris, Jonathan, and now Baby Benjamin Hendrickson, for your endless friendship and support; Arielle Ford and Brian Hilliard for looking out for me and loving my little guy as much as you do. And of course, Michael Arnold Koenigs (MAK), thank you for being the partner I can travel the limitless possibilities of life with—you continue to amaze me. It is such a joy for me to watch the miracle of you as a father—your love shines in our little boy's eyes every day.

About the Author

VIVIAN E. GLYCK is a writer, entrepreneur, and strategic marketing consultant. She is the author of *Twelve Lessons on Life I Learned from My Garden: Spiritual Guidance from the Vegetable Patch* (Rodale, 1997). She lives in San Diego with her husband and son.

Visit www.glyck.com to learn about Vivian, or visit www.TaoofPoop.com to:

- join a community of conscious mothers like you who think "outside the box"
- share your tips for staying sane while raising a baby
- receive a free monthly "Sanity Saver" newsletter
- receive a free gift just for visiting the site